Who was Lord Conyers?

by Geoff Nuttall

Front Cover illustration: *(top to bottom)*
Lords Conyers 3, 8 and 14
John Conyers, Robert Darcy, Sackville George Pelham
(Detail of John Conyers from a Private Collection/Photo courtesy of the National Portrait Gallery, London)

Shields of Arms:
Conyers, Darcy, Osborne, Lane-Fox, Pelham

Back Cover and above:
Hornby Castle, south-east aspect

Published by Geoff Nuttall
3 Broad Dyke Close, Kiveton Park, Sheffield S26 6LF

ISBN 0 9536149 0 5

Colour images by Oakleaf Graphics, Chesterfield

Printed by Dunston Printers, Chesterfield

Table of Contents

Introduction

In 1970 and coincident with the revival of public interest at that time in folk music in the United Kingdom, a thriving and predominantly traditional folk club became established at Wales, near Sheffield. The club was called the Kiveton Park Folk Club and met every Tuesday at the Lord Conyers Arms in Wales Square.

In the Autumn of 1974 a dozen men from the club decided to form themselves into a Morris Dance team and became known and publicised as Lord Conyers Morris Men. Since that time they have built up an extensive repertoire of dances collected predominantly from the Cotswold region of England, and since 1975 have travelled and performed extensively in England and occasionally in Europe.

On many occasions whilst performing, members of the team have been asked by the spectating public "who is/was Lord Conyers?" Invariably the reply was imprecise, possibly inadequate, and generally took the form of something akin to "we think he was something to do with the Duke of Leeds" or "we think he used to own a lot of the land around Kiveton". If truth be known, the team's research into Lord Conyers had been limited.

Lord Conyers Morris Men, like many organisations, hold Annual Business Meetings. In 1995, "Who was Lord Conyers?" appeared under the "Any Other Business" item on the agenda.

I hope the following casts a little light on the matter.

The reader will see how the first Lords Conyers were descended from the 11th Century legendary Conyers family of Sockburn, County Durham; then follows the progression of the Lord Conyers title by marriage from the original Conyers surname through the subsequent great families of Darcy, Osborne, Lane-Fox, and Pelham.

The story starts with the dragon-slaying legend of the ancient Conyers and its association with the factual symbolic exchange ceremony of a falchion with incoming Bishops of Durham.

Early pedigrees are reviewed and a reasoned argument put forward to identify the descent link of Conyers of Sockburn and the Lords Conyers of Hornby Castle. In chronological order, a section is dedicated to each of the fourteen Lords Conyers, including two baronesses, and their connection with other major families are examined at the appropriate stage in the text.

Their influence in the South Yorkshire area receives specific mention throughout.

It is seen how the Lords Conyers devolved from Hornby Castle near Bedale in North Yorkshire, and how they twice returned there after leaving their other South Yorkshire seats. These later Lords bore the surname not of Conyers, but of Darcy, and Osborne.

The appendices have been compiled to provide easy to look at summaries together with sections on Hornby Castle and Conyers heraldry.

The writer is a member of Lord Conyers Morris Men. It is his first attempt into local history research and there are bound to be omissions and inaccuracies, though hopefully not too many of the latter. We would be pleased to learn of any additional material which would clarify, support, otherwise embellish, or even correct what is printed here.

Please address correspondence to:-

Geoff Nuttall
3 Broad Dyke Close
Kiveton Park
Sheffield S26 6LF

E-mail: geoff@gncon.free-online.co.uk

Of Dragons & Falchions

DRAGONS

"Sr Jo Conyers of Storkburn Knt who slew ye monstrous venoms and poysons wiverms Ask or worme which overthrew and Devourd many people in fight, for the scent of the poyson was soo strong, that no person was able to abide it, yet he by the providence of god overthrew it, and lyes buryed at Storkburn before the Conquest, but before he did enterprise it (having but one sonne) he went to the Church in compleat armour and offered up his sonne to the holy ghost, which monumt is yet to see, and the place where the serpent lay is called Graystone".

The above is the earliest documented reference to the dragon-slaying Conyers and a legend commonly known as the Sockburn Worm. It is dated to the time of King Charles I (1625-1649), and is taken from a Harleian Society Manuscript at the British Museum (2).

"Worm" originates from the Norse "orm" or "ormr", meaning serpent or dragon. A wyvern is a winged two-legged dragon with barbed tail, while an aske indicates a lizard-style animal. Storkburn is the old name of Sockburn which lies in a loop of the River Tees at the southernmost tip of County Durham, about seven miles south-east of Darlington. It originated as a Saxon manor and was a major family seat of Conyers from the 12th to the 17th Century. The "Graystone" (Fig.1) is a large limestone slab which still lies in a field near Sockburn Church, having resisted all man's efforts to move it.

The monster reputedly took the milk of several cows every night, and bathed itself in a trough near the Greystone before returning to the river.

An amusing yet interesting account of how the dragon was allegedly slain is reported by Harwood Brierley in the Yorkshire Weekly Post of 21st. February 1914. Four paragraphs of this most colourful description are recorded here in full:-

"We are to suppose that one Sir John Conyers went crusading to the Holy Land with the Christianly warriors of King Richard I, surnamed "Coeur-de-Lion." We are also to suppose that when he returned home about AD 1180 he found his serfs and villeins, and, indeed, the whole countryside around his manorial fief, demoralised by the reign of terror caused by a most loathsome creature variously called a dragon, a wyvern, an aske, fiery flying serpent, vermyne, werme, or worm. This monster, which was said to be invulnerable, devoured women, maidens, and children; it exhaled poison with its breath; yet, in order to save their own skins, the terrified people

Sockburn. The 'Greystone'. (Courtesy of Joyce Cracknell)

supplied it daily with as much new milk as seven cows would yield, carrying the same to a trough at the Grey Stone which is still "in situ."

Sir John Conyers had doubtless heard tell of dragons, griffins, wyverns, and other fabulous monsters before. Modern science professes to have disproved them, yet I am not at all sure that it has disproved the great sea-serpent, which usually crosses the vision of marine tourists during the "silly season," when Parliament is not sitting. This redoubtable Sir John Conyers may even have heard tell of such terrible antediluvian beasts as the plesiosaurus, ichthysaurus, and pterodactyl, whose fossilised remains are still at times dislodged from oolitic strata. Could it be possible for any of these to have found a stronghold in the fastnesses of Sockburn in Conyers's time? I trow not. Nevertheless, the ancient monastic chroniclers could hardly fail to exaggerate any vile, venomous saurian that a Christianly champion of the oppressed set out to destroy. This doughty crusader would regard any pagan enemy of the Church as vermin, and it would pleasure him to hunt wolves and vicious wild boars of the forest. He would be the last person to preserve such a rarity as a dragon, wyvern, or aske, which had its lair on his own secluded manor.

Yet, had he not some qualms concerning his own fate at the issue of this proposed encounter? A presumably veracious chronicler informs us that Sir John Conyers had one son (possibly Galfrid, who became Vicar of Sockburn), and that, ere starting out to assail the dragon, he settled all his temporal and spiritual affairs, and went to the altar in panoply of war to "offer this one sonne to the Holy Ghost." That was considered the best possible send-off on a very dangerous errand. With a scimitar-like falchion in one hand, and a shield in the other, and a favourite hound for company, he valiantly sallied forth to the

pestilent dragon's haunt. Scenting the hound, the surprised dragon came at once out of hiding, breathed forth its noxious vapour, raised its razor-edged scales, angrily snapped its iron-hard teeth, and sought to enfold the champion. In the terrible conflict which ensued this mythical product of the natural world soon conceded to human eyes that it was not invulnerable. The doughty knight of the palatinate wielded his falchion with dexterity, hacking a way through the reptile's scales and articulations; till at last, on the famous Grey Stone, "by the providence of Almighty God, this John Conyers, knyght, overthrew the said venomous monster, and slew it." He chopped off the head and tail as trophies, and sent for his serfs to dig a hole where the Grey Stone stood, in an arable field to the westward of the church, and there the carcase was buried.

This relic of other geological ages measures about 4ft. by 2 and a half ft. Many years ago a farm tenant who found it a stumbling block in the line of his plough, determined to get rid of it. Having made a drill and inserted an explosive charge, he fused the same and abortively blew it up, a deep fissure being the testimony of this violence. With more success his landlord "blew HIM up," and removed him from the farm."

The legendary act of dragon-slaying is usually associated not only with St. George, but with a named hero of an important land-owning family, and that of Conyers was no exception. Others include Sir John Lambton, the Pollards of Bishop Auckland, Sir Piers Shonks at Brent Pelham (Herts), and Sir Hugh Barde at Castle Carlton (Lincs) (3).

It is possible that the Conyers family deliberately associated themselves with an earlier legend in order to increase their social standing within the community or to impress the all-powerful Bishops of Durham. It is also conceivable that a Conyers did in fact carry out an act of great bravery to the benefit of the local people and was rewarded with the fertile valley of Sockburn and its manor.

Certainly, the act of dragon-slaying has been a euphemism for acts of valour, as evidenced by the South Yorkshire legend in which More of More Hall kills the dragon of Wortley. This is thought to refer to an act of vengeance by George Blount against Sir Thomas Wantley who demolished settlements of houses to extend his deer park. An early example of the worm having turned!

N.B. The Pollard family are also associated, like Conyers, with a falchion exchange ceremony with incoming Bishops of Durham, and their heraldic crest is a falchion.

Sir John Conyers' valorous deed is indicated by the legend as having taken place before the Norman Conquest, and there is an unconvincing reference dating it to

1063. (See pg.12). Here again, it is possible that the Conyers family, being of Norman origin, may have introduced the pre-Conquest connotation to enhance the legend.

Dragon stories were well known in Saxon times both by the Anglo-Saxons themselves and by the Vikings, who began to settle in the Tees area in the 9th Century. It has been suggested that such stories may have been promoted to display shared values and traditions, thereby generating trust and reconciliation. Could it be that the Sockburn Worm was created for just such social reasons?(52).

Various other hypotheses have been proposed regarding the origin of the Conyers legend, one of which, being of a general nature of such stories, is that it represented victory for Christian beliefs over Saxon or Viking paganism. From a more local viewpoint it has been suggested that the victory over the dragon related to a battle success over the Scots or over a Danish invader. On a more practical basis it has been suggested that there were sulphur springs in the fields at Sockburn and that Conyers was the first to cap them, thereby eliminating the foul emissions. More plausible, however, is that the legend refers to the successful resistance to, and the eventual overthrow of William Cumyn, a Scottish usurper, by Roger Conyers in 1143. Cumyn had designs to be the Bishop of Durham with all the associated powers of that title, and went to great lengths in his attempts, including the forgery of letters from Rome and the torture of anyone who stood in his path. Some of his prisoners were suspended across ropes with heavy weights attached to the neck and feet, whilst of others, **"the naked feet, protruding through an aperture in the wall, were exposed to all the severity of the night."**(32).

Roger Conyers was the only noble of the time to resist Cumyn and his troops, and in self-defence he greatly fortified his manor-house at Bishopton, a few miles from Sockburn. At this time Cumyn was spreading everywhere **"terror and destruction"** and had sacked Durham town and Abbey.

Thus, the eventual defeat of Cumyn would have been a great conquest for Roger Conyers when other barons had deserted him, albeit some assistance was provided to him in the later stages by two other barons of the Bishopric, Galfrid de Escolland and Bertram Bulmer. He had maintained his allegiance to the true Bishop of Durham, William Ste Barbe, provided him with shelter at this time, and against all odds allowed the Bishop to take up his rightful seat. Nor did Conyers finish the contest in the usual manner by killing Cumyn, but brought him, as Surtees describes, **"a humble kneeling penitent before the Episcopal throne."** (1).

FALCHIONS

"Sockburn, where Conyers so trusty
A huge serpent did dish up,
That had else eat the Bish-up,
But now his old faulchion's grown rusty, grown rusty."

This literary gem is from an article by W.H.Longstaffe in the Durham Advertiser of 24th November 1848, in which he is writing about the legendary traditions of County Durham. It serves as a convenient link between the dragon slaying legend and the falchion exchange ceremony with new Bishops of Durham.

There are reports that the Conyers were a Saxon family who named themselves after their favourite flower or plant, as was the custom at one time. Thus Conyers is synonymous with the quince plant.

Nevertheless, the Conyers family are generally regarded as being of Norman origin having come over with the Conqueror, and settled in the North-East of England.

Various spellings of Conyers are encountered in manuscripts and past records, some of the others being: Congrues (as indicated to travel writer John Leland by a Conyers of Sockburn himself), Connyers, Coniers, Coisners, Coiniers, Coygnyers, Coigniers, Connieres, Cogniers, Coigners, Coyners, Coyner, Conyre.

The name is usually regarded to mean "coin-maker".

The Conyers were well-favoured henchmen of the Conqueror and after the Conquest were granted extensive land and titles in County Durham and North Yorkshire, despite the pillaging inflicted on that part of the country.

Bowes manuscripts (1) state that **"Roger Conyers was by William the Conqueror made Constable of Durham Castle and Keeper of all the armes of ye souldiers within the Castle, wh was after past to him ye saide Roger by deede to him and his heires mailes for ever, under the great seale of William de Sancto Carilepho, Bishop of Durham"**. This is the first historical mention of the Conyers family and presumably refers to a time before the Conqueror's death in 1087.

In the earliest days the Conyers were Lords of the Manor at Bishopton, several miles North-East of Darlington, and of Sockburn. In fact, the earliest charters refer to Bishopton, one of which is remarkable with its reference to slave-trading.

This is described in Surtees as being **"the grant by Roger Conyers, of Thomas and Turstine, sons of Eylof, of Biscoptun, with all their sequel, to**

the Church, for a horse and six marks, with which Roger had been supplied in his utmost need by the Treasury of St. Cuthbert. A charger, probably, and money for a campaign, be it in Scotland or Palestine, and which was paid for by transferring the very bodies and liberties of his serfs, with all the slave-born issue of their loins".

St. Cuthbert was bishop of Lindisfarne 685-687A.D. and his remains lie under Durham Cathedral.

Most pedigrees of the Conyers family start with a Roger Conyers at the time of the Conqueror but one pedigree (5) indicates this Roger to be the son of Sir John Conyers who slew the dragon allegedly in 1063.

Ranulf Flambard was Bishop of Durham from 1099 to 1128 and it was he who granted the Lordships of Sockburn, Rungeton (Yorks) and Hutton Conyers to Roger, son of the above Roger. He also inherited the Constableship of Durham Castle and Beckwith (5) confirms this inheritance in which Roger is attired in **"compleat armour, sustaining his faucheon and shield."**

Bishop Flambard was the Minister and advisor to William Rufus who was the younger son of the Conqueror, although Flambard is described as of lowly origin and referred to by monks as the son of a pagan or witch. (6). A holy man indeed!

The next in the Conyers line was a third Roger who, along with other families, successfully thwarted the Scottish usurper Cumyn, and as indicated earlier, provided the Bishop of Durham, William Ste Barbe (Bishop from 1143-1152), a safe retreat in his Bishopton Peel-house.

Thus the arrangements became clear that in exchange for land tenure the Lords of the manors provided the Bishops with military protection.

With regards to the incoming Bishops of Durham, a ceremonial custom evolved whereby on the entry of the new Bishop from the South into his Prince Bishopric and Diocese, a falchion, or broad-pointed sword, was exchanged with the Lord of the Manor of Sockburn. The ceremony originally took place in the middle of the river Tees at the ford leading across to Over Dinsdale, or at Neasham Ford. In high river conditions, and latterly, the ceremony would take place in the middle of the road bridge at Croft-on-Tees. (Plate 1) By custom the falchion was presented to the incoming Bishop by the senior Conyers of the day as an emblem of the Bishop's temporal power. For his part the exchange represented Conyers' continued allegiance, and as a sign that he recognised the Bishop as overlord from whom he held his estate. The falchion is thus regarded as a tenure sword, and by this symbolic act the privilege of the manorial right was held.

There is a claim that the ceremony may date back to the time of Bishop Hugh Pudsey (Hugh of Le Puiset) in 1153 (3), and also an implication that it was performed even earlier in 1099 to Bishop Ranulf Flambard by Roger Conyers (9), although the latter claim would pre-date the Cumyn/Roger Conyers confrontation.

Certainly the ceremony is unequivocally documented in the Inquisitions Post Mortem on Sir John Conyers taken 6th March 1395-96 and 2nd April 1397 at Durham. Both state that Sir John held the Manor of Sockburn by the service of showing a falchion.

The wording as used by the Conyers, Lord of Sockburn Manor, is quoted as follows by Surtees and Hutchinson, and reproduced in Wall. (4).

"My Lord Bishop, I hereby present you with the Falchion whereby the champion Conyers slew the Worm, Dragon, or Fiery Flying Serpent, which destroyed man, woman and child, in memory of which the King then reigning gave him the Manor of Sockburn, to hold by this tenure, that, upon the first entrance of every Bishop into this County, this falchion should be presented". The Bishop takes the falchion in his hand, then immediately returns it, wishing the Lord of Sockburn good health and a long enjoyment of the Manor.

Thereby the link is established between the dragon-slaying Conyers legend and the medieval land tenureship ceremony. The custom continued throughout the Conyers ownership of the Sockburn Manor, their descendents and subsequent owners. The branch of the Sockburn Conyers that were the ancestors of the Lords Conyers left Sockburn towards the end of the 14th Century, so the Lords Conyers themselves (of Hornby) would not be involved in the ceremony.

In 1635 William Conyers of Sockburn died without male issue but his younger daughter became the wife of Francis Talbot, Earl of Shrewsbury in which family the Sockburn Manor was vested. In 1666 the presentation to the incoming Bishop was carried out by Mr. William Collingwood, Steward and Tenant of the Talbots. Prior to 1685 the Sockburn estate became owned by Sir William Blackett of Newcastle, presumably as a result of being sold by the Talbots. The Blacketts, who were wealthy colliery owners, later built Newby Hall in Yorkshire, but sold that property in 1748.

Sir Edward Blackett presented the falchion to Bishop John Egerton in 1771, and John Erasmus Blackett presented it on behalf of his brother Sir Edward, to Bishop Thomas Thurlow in 1787.

The wording of the address in 1787 as recorded by Sharp (8), and reproduced in John Wall's article is as follows -

"Sir Edward Blackett, Bart., now represents the person of Sir John Conyers who in the year 1063, in the field of Sockburn, with this falchion, slew a monstrous creature, a dragon, a worm, or a flying serpent, that devoured men, women and children. The owner of Sockburn, as a reward for his bravery, gave him the manor, with its appurtenances, for him and his heirs, to hold forever, on condition that he meets the Lord Bishop of Durham, with this falchion, on his first entrance into his Diocese after his first appointment to that fee."

His Lordship was then said to have received and returned the falchion "with many handsome compliments."

The wording of the address at this time is specific with respect to "1063" and "this falchion", and maybe without foundation in this regard.

The last occasion the traditional ceremony took place on Croft road bridge was 1826 when the steward of Sir Edward Blackett presented the falchion to Dr. William Van Mildert, though in 1860 a private ceremony was performed to Bishop Villiers when his train stopped on Croft railway bridge on the Tees.

This would have been in sharp contrast to most of the earlier occasions which were public affairs to which the gentry and populace resorted in large numbers, for example in 1661 when John Cosin became Bishop. Miles Stapleton's letter to William Sancroft of August 22, 1661 describes the scene:-

"As soon as he came in sight of the river banks, the trumpets sounded, and the gentry, with the troops of horse, all in one body, judged to be about 1,000, moved into the midst of the river, where, when my Lord came, the usual ceremony of delivering a great drawne faulchion was performed, after which the trumpets sounded againe, and great acclamation of the people followed: which ended, they proceeded in order to Darlington."

Bishop Cosin's own account, also addressed to William Sancroft, confirms the popularity of the occasion.

"At my first entrance through the river of Tease, there was scarce any water to be seene for the multitude of horse and men yt filled it, when ye sword yt killed ye dragone was delivered to me with all the formality of trumpets and gunshots and acclamations yt might be made."

This particular ceremony would have been without Conyers participation in the presentation since the last of the male Sockburn line had died some 26 years earlier.

Bishop Jenkins accepts the Conyers falchion in September 1984. (Picture courtesy of The Northern Echo.)

Attempts to have the custom revived in the early 20th Century were unsuccessful, and it was to be 1984 before the falchion was used again in the ceremony.

In 1973 Bishop Habgood undertook the ceremonial walk over Croft bridge to be greeted by the Rectors of Hurworth and Darlington but the falchion could not be used, ostensibly to protect its condition.

The ancient custom has now been revived, though with a much modernised script. In September 1984 the ceremony was held on Croft Bridge where the falchion was presented by the Mayor of Darlington, Mr Philip Stamford-Bewlay to Bishop David Jenkins.(Fig.2)

The Bishop said he looked forward to fighting the dragons of unemployment, conflict and apathy.

It was last performed in September 1994 when the participants were Darlington's Mayor, Mr John Williams, and the current Bishop, Michael Turnbull.

THE CONYERS FALCHION

The falchion was normally kept at Sockburn Manor House but was presented to the Dean and Chapter of Durham Cathedral in 1947 by Mr. Arthur Edward Blackett. It is now preserved there in the Treasury as one of its prized possessions. (Plate 1)

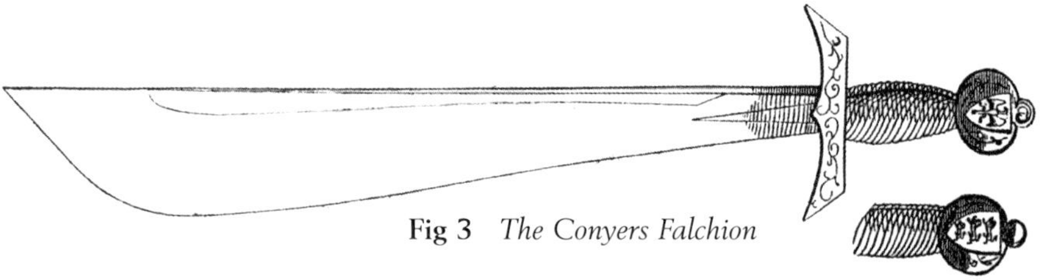

Fig 3 *The Conyers Falchion*

Despite falchions appearing in numerous early illustrations, the Conyers falchion is one of only eight preserved in Europe, there being two others in England. It is dated at 1260-1270, some two centuries after the alleged dragon-slaying performance of John Conyers, and it may be a replacement copy of an earlier one.

This imposing weapon is 89cm (almost 3ft) long, the blade itself being 74cm, and is 11.5cm wide at its broadest. The appearance of the blade suggests it has been frequently ground and cleaned, and shows evidence of some rough usage, indicating it was not used solely for ceremonial purposes. The falchion's bronze pommel has shields of Arms on both sides, one bearing in red enamel the Arms of the Plantagenet Kings of England from Henry II (1154-1189) to Edward III (1327-1377). The other side shows a black eagle with raised wings, the fictional Arms of Morcar, the Saxon Earl of Northumberland. This Imperial eagle was later adopted by Henry III and his younger brother and half-brother. It is these heraldic associations along with the stylistic evidence that have helped to project the falchion's late 13th Century date. The bronze guard (16.8cm long) is decorated appropriately with winged biting serpents having interlaced bodies and tails.

Fig 4
The Conyers Falchion Pommel and Guard detail. (The Dean and Chapter of Durham)

SOCKBURN

The peace and solitude of Sockburn, along with its verdant green pastures and the flowing Tees must have been very attractive to the Conyers, since it was here, despite the heroics at Bishopton that they established their first major family seat in the 12th Century.

Fig 5

Sockburn Hall. Built for the Blacketts in 1835

Lying seven miles south by south-east of Darlington and accessible only by the single track lane proceeding south from Neasham, Sockburn is almost isolated from the rest of the community by the river Tees which flows in a loop around it.

As the lane degenerates into a rough track the first-time visitor wonders what will greet him at its end, but suddenly, from behind the trees and at the bottom of a slight decline, the dark imposing Hall comes into view.

This Gothic-style building was erected in 1835 for the Blackett family, whose shield of arms is carved in stone above the entrance. According to Bulmer's Directory the Hall was standing empty by 1890, though it is occupied nowadays.

The current Hall has no connection with the Conyers apart from the fact that the Blacketts purchased the estate from the Talbots prior to 1685. The Talbots had become owners by the marriage of Anne Conyers to Francis Talbot, Earl of Shrewsbury. Anne's father William died in 1635 and was the last male Conyers at Sockburn.

The Hall stands very close to the site of the original Conyers home, and nearby, through the undergrowth, stand the ruined arches of Sockburn Church together with the preserved section that houses the remaining Conyers monuments. Curiously, there is a much older monument in the Church, a 10th Century Viking gravestone or hogback which shows a man surrounded by beasts. This is believed to depict the battle between the Norse God, Tyr, and a savage giant wolf called Fenyr. Another twist to the tale of the Sockburn Worm?

The traveller and writer John Leland visited Sockburn some time in the 16th Century and was presumably a guest of the Conyers at that time. He describes the area as **"exceedingly pleasant ground"** with good fishing in the river.

Earlier still, in the 15th Century, the Manor and Manor-house contained a Hall, chamber, kitchen, granary, stable, dovecote, three orchards, three cottages with their gardens, a water mill, an enclosed wood, and both arable and meadowland.

The pastures seemed particularly suitable for rearing sheep and cattle, as records indicate that in 1777 Mr. Thomas Hutchinson of Sockburn bred a sheep weighing 17 stones 8lbs. (112Kg.), and in 1822 a John Hutchinson published "The Origin and Pedigree of the Sockburne Short Horns". The Hutchinson's owned Sockburn Farm, and two sisters, Mary and Sara fell in love here with the poets Wordsworth and Coleridge respectively. Mary and Wordsworth were later wed but Coleridge was already married. Another traveller-writer/herald to visit Sockburn was James Dugdale in 1666 in which he describes various armorial decorations that were in the Hall at that time. The resident then was Mr. William Collingwood, steward of the Talbots. At some time during the ownership of the Blacketts, the Hall was dismantled, or as the current occupant of the 1835 Sockburn Hall suggests, it fell into the river.

In any event, as Robert Surtees observed in 1823, **"of the house of the Conyers not one stone is now left on another."** (1)

SOCKBURN CHURCH

There was a church here in Saxon times where Higbald was consecrated Bishop of Lindisfarne in 780. The earliest recorded Rector is "Galfrid de Connieres" in 1168. To quote further from Surtees in 1823, "The little church, standing lonely on its level green, has survived the halls of its ancient patrons". The Old Hall stood a little to the south and at that time could be seen traces of foundations of gardens and orchards.

Fig 6

Sockburn Church, showing the ruins of the chancel and the preserved chapel

The parish of Sockburn includes the villages of Girsby and High Dinsdale on the south side of the Tees, and therefore these parishioners had to ford the river, or cross by boat to attend Church. Thus, inconveniently situated to most, and becoming in a dilapidated condition, in 1835 a new Church was built on the south side of the river which led to the partial demolition of the old one.

The passing of the old Church was much lamented by some and this is probably best expressed by the Rev. James Raine:- **"But it has been removed because, by no fault of its own, it stood in front of a newly-erected mansion house, and the various old monuments in brass or stone in commemoration of its Lords, which it contained within its walls, have disappeared. Thus has been desecrated, and converted to common and profane uses, that holy place, in which had been offered up to the throne of grace, from generation to generation, the prayers and praise of a pious people; in which had been administered for centuries**

the blessed sacrament of the body and blood of Christ; in which the children of the little district had been suffered to come to their Saviour by the regenerating layer of baptism; in which had been plighted the marriage vow; and which had received into its protecting bosom the remains of the dead, the seeds of immortality.

What a strange fatality attaches itself to the house of Conyers! The name is gone and so are its memorials".

1835 must have been a busy year for the Blacketts, erecting a new Hall, a new Church which they part financed, and part demolishing the old Church. They did, however, preserve part of the old Church, the small chancel that housed the Conyers graves. The main artefacts still remaining are a stone effigy of a knight and four blue marble floor slabs with inlaid brass inscriptions. The knightly effigy (Plate 1) is estimated to be late 13th Century - early 14th Century and is fully armoured, with chain-work helmet. The sword is being unsheathed from its scabbard below the blank shield. The crossed feet with spurs on the heels rest on a lion which has in its mouth a winged serpent, no doubt alluding to the dragon legend.

Fig 7

Sculpturing on the memorial of Sir John Conyers (d.1395) at Sockburn Church

Of the marble memorials on the floor, the one nearest the current entrance doorway is that of Sir John Conyers who died 1395 and at whose inquest reference was made to his participation in the falchion ceremony. His slab is sculptured with a cross flory, a sword, and the arms of Conyers. (Fig.7)

The adjacent memorial is that of John's son Robert Conyers, who died in 1433, and his wife Isabella Pert. The wooden cover of the font bears Conyers shields quartering some of the families of their wives (Vesey, from Elizabeth de Aton who married the Sir John Conyers mentioned above; Markenfield, from Anne who married Christopher Conyers in 1487; and a Scrope/Tiptoft combination from the above Isabella, granddaughter of Stephen Scrope).

As the old Church lies on private land, would-be visitors are advised to make arrangements in advance with the owner at Sockburn Hall.

HUTTON CONYERS AND NORTON CONYERS

Family seats at the above places soon followed that at Sockburn. At Hutton, as at Sockburn, "not one stone is now left on another".

The Hall at Hutton Conyers was believed to have been moated and lay just to the north of the village in a field called Hallgarth.

Norton Conyers now consists entirely of the Jacobean house owned for nearly four hundred years by the Graham family, and is a prime candidate to have been Thornfield Hall in Charlotte Bronte's Jane Eyre. Yet the earliest parts of this house go back to the mid-14th Century when it was home to the Conyers. A small village developed by the house, and a church once occupied the position where the clock tower now stands.

Following the marriage of Roger Conyers and Margaret Norton in the 14th Century, this branch of the Conyers family changed their name to Norton. They rebuilt the house about 1500, making it plain brick with a flat battlemented roof and arrow-slits in the walls, traces of which can still be seen. The rough-cast which covers the brick is a much later addition, and though there have been many other additions, the essential structure remains unchanged. The curved gables were added in 1632.

In 1569 the Norton family joined with the Earls of Westmorland and Northumberland in the unsuccesful plot to depose Queen Elizabeth I, and all their estates became confiscated by the Crown.

Norton Conyers was sold to the Musgrave family, and in 1624 it was bought by the Graham family following the marriage of Catherine Musgrave to Richard Graham.

The house is still owned, and lived in, by the Grahams. At certain times of the year it is open to the public.

Norton Conyers. (Courtesy of Sir James Graham)

Early Pedigrees - to 1400

The purpose of this section is to trace the two main descents through Sockburn and Norton/Hutton Conyers and is to investigate the link with John Conyers, the first of the family at Hornby Castle.

There is evidence of a Conyers murdering his elder brother at the end of the 12th Century and conflicting accounts of just where the Hornby ancestor John Conyers fits into the family pedigree. The conflicting pedigrees are examined and the favoured option is presented.

On examination of the early descents it is not surprising that discrepancies arise since record-keeping was not formalised and errors can occur as a result of assumption, mis-transposition or lack of accurate information. Nevertheless a good deal of commonality does exist, and a presentation of three options follows, covering the two main branches to 1400.

CONYERS
The Early Major Pedigrees to 1400

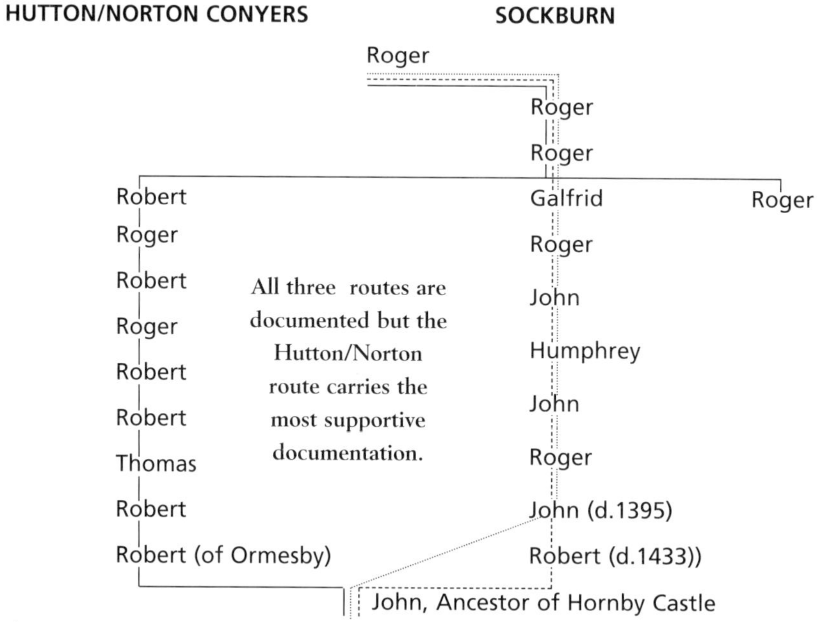

The preceding descents are obviously simplified and omit brothers and all descendencies through the Norton Conyers/Hutton Conyers line at Cotherston, Angodby, Warton (Lancs), Yeland Conyers (Lancs), Finingham, Wald Newton, Heghe (Northumberland), and Clifton.

In determining whether it is the later Sockburn line or the earlier branch through Hutton/Norton that supplies the first Conyers at Hornby, it is necessary to study the evidence, primarily in terms of dates.

Both Beckwith (5) and Burke (9) in their Conyers pedigrees claim that Robert Conyers of Sockburn had four sons, and that the fourth son was John, originator of the Hornby Castle line *(dashed line opposite)*. The Harleian Manuscript 4198 "Yorkshire Arms and Descents" also indicates this. Whilst they do not provide dates, Surtees' pedigree does, showing this Robert was born 1371 and died 1433. His monument lies in Sockburn Church. Robert's eldest son, Christopher, lived around 1422 - 1487, implying that any fourth son could not have been born before 1425. It is known that four generations down from John of Hornby, the first Lord Conyers lived from 1468 - 1524. Four generations, well documented to prove their veracity, cannot be accommodated within the 43 years from 1425 to 1468.

There is supportive evidence elsewhere, ie:-

a) Hopkinson's narrative (12) refers to an article in Hollinshead Chronicles of 1389 stating John Conyers, a Judge, became Lord of Hornby as a result of his marriage to Margaret St. Quintin of Hornby. Even had John been Robert's first son, he could only have been born about this date, let alone have the maturity to be a Judge.

b) The Hornby Church Handbook (13) states that John Conyers built the south aisle of the Church in 1409.

c) Beckwith refers to John Conyers, a Judge, being a great friend of Richard Lord Scrope in the time of Edward III. Edward III reigned 1327 - 1377 and Richard Lord Scrope died in 1403.

These points confirm by virtue of the early date references that John would not have been the son of Robert of Sockburn.

This John, therefore, must be of an older generation and it would be logical to suggest that he is one generation further back down the Sockburn line, i.e. the brother of Robert (d.1433), not his son *(dotted line)*. In this case he would have been son of John who married into the de Aton /Lord Vesey family; (see Appendix 2 on Conyers heraldry). Certainly there is a piece of documented evidence to support this theory, from the Clay collection of

Yorkshire Pedigrees held by The Yorkshire Archaeological Society in Leeds. Although the content is sparse and lacks supportive corroboration, this does not mean it can be completely discounted.

Harrison's pedigree (35) does, however, provide a well-documented and viable alternative, showing the origination from the Sockburn parent trunk back in the 12th Century through the Norton and Hutton Conyers branch *(solid line)*. As well as providing a full and detailed account of the descents of early Conyers, this pedigree shows that John of Hornby died in 1413, thereby confirming the older generation status required.

Further corroborative evidence of the derivation through Harrison's pedigree lies with Flower (33), where a footnote states that Sir Robert Conyers born in 1325, died in 1392, and a descendent from Hutton Conyers, was father of John Conyers of Hornby, husband to the heiress of St. Quintin. This latter fact is also stated in Tonge's visitation (34).

Having established the probable descent link from the oldest Sockburn branch via Hutton/Norton it is worthwhile to consider in a little more detail the descent route from the time of William the Conqueror. Assuming the family were of Norman origin, this will provide continuity from these earliest days, through to Hornby Castle and the subsequent Lords Conyers.

Fig 9

Hornby Castle c. 1720. From a sketch by Samuel Buck (Wakefield Historical Publications)

Conyers Descent Pedigree

Roger (to 1090)

He came into England at the time of the Conquest and was made Constable of Durham Castle and Governor of the garrison there by William Rufus, the Conqueror's son. This act was made under the seal of William de Sancto CaripheIo, Bishop of Durham.

Sir Roger (early 12C)

Bishop Ranulf Flambard (Bishop 1099 - 1128) gave him the Yorkshire manor of Rungeton. He was also Lord of "Howton Coigniers" and Sockburn. He inherited the Constableship of Durham Castle by a deed of 1102 and was married to Emma, daughter of Ralph Aslaby.

Sir Roger (living 1143, 1172)

He was a baron of the Bishopric of Durham and Lord of Bishopton and "Howton Coigniers". With his eldest son Robert he gave the Churches of Sockburn, where his brother Galfrid was Rector in 1168, and Bishopton, to Sherburn House Hospital (Durham). He gave land to the Church at Neasham. It was this Roger that overthrew the usurper Cumyn, which story might have been the foundation of the dragon-slaying legend (see earlier section under "Dragons"). He was married twice; to Mary, who was mother to the three sons below, and to Basilia.

Robert, Galfrid, Roger

Sir Robert, eldest son of Roger, though Beckwith's pedigree implies he is his brother. He was Lord of Hutton Conyers but is said to have been defrauded of his lands and killed by his younger brother Roger shortly after returning from a Holy Land Crusade in the company of Richard I. This occurred before 1195, and he left a widow, Mabilla.

Galfrid or Geoffrey. The name was sometimes written as Galfridus in old Latin chronicles, which led to the 19th Century pseudo-antique name Galfrid. He was a younger brother of Robert and was married to Alicia, sister to Adam de Yeland, though some pedigrees state he was married to Elinor, daughter of Hugh Lithorne. He was Constable of Durham Castle in 1221, and Lord of Bishopton and Sockburn as a result of his surviving both his brothers. He died in 1230 and from him came the long line of Sockburn Conyers' up to the 17th Century.

Roger. Having claimed the land of his eldest brother Robert, a feud arose between this Roger and the nephew Roger (below), son of Robert. This was settled before the Kings Justices at Westminster in 1195 where the above Roger was granted the Bishopton, Sockburn, Stainton, Rungeton, Auckland and Dinsdale lands i.e. most of them, and nephew Roger took the manor of Fylingham (or Finingham) in Suffolk. Roger died without issue and these lands then passed to Galfrid above.

Sir Roger (died before 1238)

Roger was dissatisfied with the above arrangements with his uncle and in 1196 paid the King 40 marks to review it. He also paid a further sum of 15 marks for an investigation into the death of his father, with which he charged his uncle Roger. It would seem he had good reason to have felt badly done by.

The reference to murder is manifest only in the Harrison pedigree, while others refer to Roger having sold his inheritance to his uncle but without explanation why. He was married to Hugelesia, daughter of Sir Ivo de Longvillers, Lord of Hoton Longvillers, Yorkshire, and of Hornby Castle, Lancashire. (This is unconnected with Hornby Castle, North Yorkshire). His younger brother William formed the Cotherston branch of the family.

Sir Robert (died before 1250)

He was Lord of Hutton Conyers and Norton Conyers. Being under-age in 1220 the Bishop of Durham assigned him to the custody of Adam de Yeland (of what is now Yealand Conyers near Carnforth, Lancashire.) He married Alicia, daughter of Nicholas, who was son of Adam de Yeland, and is recorded as being a juryman at Lancaster assizes in1245.

Sir Roger (died before 1279)

Lord of Hutton Conyers, Norton Conyers and claimed the lands in Cotherston on the death of his kinsman William. He married Agatha, daughter of Ralph de Newby. His brother Adam (of Yealand) inherited the manor of Finingham.

Sir Robert (living 1278 and 1302)

He claimed damages for waste in his lands at Norton Conyers and Norton-juxta-Wath. He married Margery, daughter of Nicholas Ward, Lord of Sallay, Yorkshire.

Sir Robert (died 1345)

He was Lord of the townships of Hutton, Norton, Holme, Hougrave, and Dinsdale, and in 1318 one of the Kings Justices Itinerant. Being appointed as one of the Commissioners of Array in the north he was commanded to certify the names of persons liable to take the degree of Knighthood. He married Emme, daughter of Hugh de Hougrave, Lord of Hougrave.

Thomas

His father gave him the manor of Dinsdale in 1333, but he was described as "of Hougrave" and living there in 1334.

Sir Robert (living 1353)

In 1333 his grandfather gave him the manors of Hutton Conyers and Norton Conyers. It is at this stage in the pedigree that the manors of Hutton and Norton become split. This Robert gave Hutton manor to his daughter Johanne and her husband Sir Christopher Mallory, and in 1353 lands in Norton to William, his son by a second marriage.

His first wife, according to Harrison was Johanna, daughter of Sir Henry Melton, niece of William Melton, Archbishop of York from 1317 to 1340.

The manor of Norton Conyers passed briefly to Richard, Lord Scrope, then to Sir Richard Conyers who by this time had changed his surname to Norton as a result of the marriage of his grandfather, Roger Conyers, to Margaret Norton. (N.B. The Conyers-Norton marriage is not indicated by Harrison, but is mentioned in most of the other pedigrees.)

Richard Norton, Lord Chief Justice of the Common Pleas in 1413 was cousin, according to Harrison, of John Conyers of Hornby and an executor of his will. This Norton surname, though strictly Conyers, still exists in the direct line of descent. In 1782 Fletcher Norton became Baron Grantley of Markenfield, and his descendents, still holding the Grantley barony, live at Markenfield Hall near Ripon. Their shield of arms is still that of the old Conyers of Norton Conyers. Their motto, appropriately enough, is "Avi Numerantur Avorum", meaning "I follow a long line of ancestry."

Sir Robert (1325 - 1392)

By his father's second wife, un-named by Harrison, but possibly Marion, daughter of Sir William Daniel and Lucie, daughter of Sir Thomas Aslakeby. (33, p.369).

He is sometimes said to be 'of Hornby', but was not associated with Hornby Castle, and may have been a tenant of Richard, Lord Scrope.

He married Juliana, daughter and heir of Sir William de Percy, Lord of Ormesby and Kildale. His two sons by this marriage were Sir Robert Conyers, Lord of Ormesby and Kildale in 1390, and John, Lord of Hornby Castle. Sir Robert was one of the executors to his brother's will in 1414.

The elder Robert was also married to Alianna de la Ley, widow of the lord of Dalden, and they had a daughter Joan who was married, in turn, to Sir Robert Bowes, Sir John Fauconberg and Thomas Bromflete.

Robert

John of Hornby (Hornby Castle Ancestor) (d.1413)

Robert (living 1390, d.1432) had a son John (of Ormesby) who had a son Robert (also of Ormesby) who had a daughter Anne. She married into the Strangways family who became Lords of Ormesby, Cleveland.

Whilst the descent quoted is that of Harrison, both Flower and Tonge indicate Joan Melton is John's mother by his father's first marriage, and that Juliana Percy and Alianna de la Ley were his father's second and third wives respectively. This argument carries some weight since the Melton's badge was a trefoil, and the Conyers of Hornby adopted it as a second crest or badge. According to Tonge this crest was once evident "both in glass and stone" in Hornby Church. Of certainty is that a trefoil is carved into the keep (south-east tower) at Hornby Castle today (Fig.31).

Both Harrison and Foster indicate the Melton - Conyers marriage to be in place in 1333, ostensibly too early for the Sir Robert Conyers who was born in 1325. Yet it is known that Archbishop Melton bought the marriage of his daughter from the Conyers family for 60 marks, and it may be that this "purchase" took place in 1333. The marriage to Juliana Percy took place about 1360, and it is proposed that she was the mother of the first Conyers at Hornby, as shown below:-

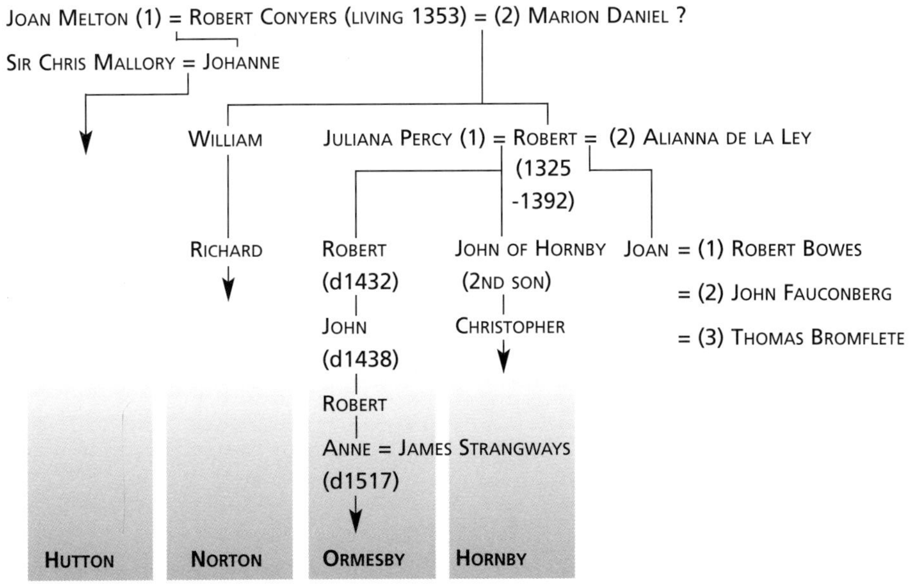

To add further weight to the above descent route, irrespective of John of Hornby's mother, Harrison reports Robert of Ormesby (d.1432) as being one of the executors to the will of his brother, John Conyers of Hornby, 1413/4. Another executor is stated to be his cousin, Sir Richard Norton (nee Conyers), Lord Chief Justice of the Common Pleas in 1413. Additionally, John of Ormesby (d.1438), is reported by Tonge to have made his cousin, Christopher Conyers of Hornby an executor to his will in 1438.

Supportive documentation to this latter part of the pedigree can be found in references (45),(46),(47).

Yet a further piece in the jigsaw is provided by the North Yorkshire County Record Office where there is a bond dated 1395 Christmas Eve "to Robert Conyers, Knt, and his brother John". There are no other obvious Robert/John brothers recorded around this time.

N.B. Some pedigrees e.g. Foster, Whitaker, indicate Sir Richard Norton (nee Conyers) to be the son of Adam Conyers and Alice Nunwych; and Adam Conyers to be the son of Roger Conyers and Margaret Norton, and not son of William as quoted by Harrison above.

It is seen that the 14th Century, particularly its later part, was a time of great significance for the Conyers family. Hutton Conyers and Norton Conyers became split, Hutton passing to the Mallory family, the Norton Conyers branch continuing, but changing their name to Norton. The Conyers lines at Ormesby and Hornby became established at this time, the Hornby line soon to outgrow in historical significance the continuing parent trunk line at Sockburn.

The St. Quintins

The St. Quintin family acquired the Hornby Manor from the De Hornby family early in the 14th Century. They were a younger branch of the St. Quintins of Harpham, all being descendants of Sir Herbert St. Quintin, one of the companions in Arms of the Conqueror.

A very brief descent at Hornby from William, nephew of Thomas St. Quintin of Hornby is:-

William St. Quintin = Joan Thweng (or Elizabeth)

John St. Quintin = Agnes Warren

Anthony St. Quintin = Elizabeth Gascoigne

Margaret St. Quintin = **John Conyers**

This shows that Anthony St.Quintin left a daughter and heir, Margaret. Margaret's wardship and marriage belonged to Richard, Lord Scrope and he married her to John Conyers, a "servant" of his in wardship, believed to be the second son of Robert Conyers of Ormesby (1325-1392).

In these medieval times it was common practice for sons of major families to enter into the families of neighbouring peers for education and the acquisition of feudal manners, so it is not suggestive that the status of the Conyers family was any less than that of St. Quintin or even Scrope. The Conyers - St. Quintin marriage took place towards the end of the 14th Century.

The Scropes

It is useful at this stage to highlight a few connections between the Scrope family and that of Conyers.

The above mentioned Richard Lord Scrope was the first Baron Scrope of Bolton Castle, Wensleydale, which he built from 1379 to 1399.

This Richard lived from 1327 to 1403, and during his time he was Lord Treasurer of England, joint warden of the West Marches, and he served with John of Gaunt in France and Scotland.

His son by his second wife was Stephen, Lord of Bentley near Doncaster. Stephen was the grandfather of Robert Conyers of Sockburn (1371-1433) by virtue of his daughter Joan marrying William Pert, whose own daughter Isabel married Robert.

A third connection down the Scrope generations shows that Mary, daughter of the 5th Lord Scrope, married William, the first Lord Conyers. She was his first wife.

This is summarised as follows:-

Blanche de la Pole (1) = **Richard**, 1st.Lord Scrope = (2) Margaret Montfort
(had wardship of John Conyers and Margaret St. Quintin)

Margaret Tibetot = **Roger**, 2nd.Lord Scrope | **Stephen**, Lord of Bentley = Millicent Tibetot

Richard, 3rd Lord Scrope | **Joan** = Wm. Pert

Henry, 4th Lord Scrope | Isabel = ***Robert Conyers*** *(of Sockburn)*

Joan Fitzhugh (1) = **John**, 5th Lord Scrope = (2)Elizabeth St. John

Mary = ***William Lord Conyers*** (1468-1524)

Hunter (18) and Foster (48) indicate that Mary's mother was the 5th Lord Scrope's second wife Elizabeth St. John, but The Complete Peerage (19), states that she was by his first wife Joan Fitzhugh, daughter of Lord Fitzhugh of Ravensworth, near Richmond.

Descent of Conyers of Hornby Castle

A simplistic descent is shown below:-

1. SIR JOHN CONYERS (d.1413)
2. SIR CHRISTOPHER CONYERS (d.1459+)
3. SIR JOHN CONYERS (d.1490)
4. SIR JOHN CONYERS (d.1469)
5. WILLIAM, 1ST LORD CONYERS (1468-1524)
6. CHRISTOPHER, 2ND LORD CONYERS (d.1538)
7. JOHN, 3RD LORD CONYERS (1523-1557)

1. Sir John Conyers

From the household of Lord Scrope, he was a judge (Chief Justice), Knight, and married the sole heiress of Hornby Castle, Margaret St. Quintin. Alabaster figures in Hornby Church could well represent them as the dress suggests a late 14th Century or early 15th Century date. He built the south aisle of Hornby Church in 1409 (Plate 2), and died in 1413 (some sources state 1422), usually being accredited with just one son, Christopher. However, a deed of 1412 names Richard and Thomas as sons, and also confirms his brother as Sir Robert. His wife survived him by a good few years as she was still living in 1426.

2. Sir Christopher Conyers

He married twice, and was prolific by both wives. His first wife was Helena Rylestone who died in 1443, but not before giving birth to 19 children according to the interpretation of Whitaker's pedigree. Whilst Sibill, Hawise, Ralph and James (or Jacob) died young, the marriages of the others are summarised on the next page.

Brasses to commemorate the lives of Christopher and Helena are laid in the floor of the South Chapel at St. Mary's Parish Church, Hornby. His will of 1426 requested he be **"buryed in the Kirk of Hornby besid my fader's tombe, whose saule God assoyle."** (Assoyle = absolve from sin).

It is worthy of note that at this stage the first two Conyers - Darcy intermarriages have been recorded, although the Darcy heiresses are not immediately related.

Christopher Conyers (living 1459)
+ Helena Rylestone (died 1443)

- **SIR JOHN CONYERS** of Hornby (1st son and heir)
  = Margerie Darcy daughter and co-heir of Philip, 6th Lord Darcy de Knayth
- **Robert** of Hutton Bonville
  = Margaret Darcy, daughter and co-heir of Sir Rowland Darcy of Hinton, Lincolnshire.
- **Sir Richard** of Cowton
  = Alice Wycliffe; he built Cowton Castle.
- **Sir Roger** of Winyard
  = Sibill (or Isabel) Langton
- **William** of Marske, Richmond
  = Elizabeth, daughter of Robert Cleesby.
- **Thomas**
- **George** of Danby Wiske
  = Isabel Franke
- **Christopher**, a priest, he further endowed the Chantry at Hornby.
- **Margaret**
  = (1) Roger Lascelles
  = (2) James Pickering
- **Johan**
  = John Fitz Randolph of Spennithorne
- **Katherine**
  = (1) Conan Aske
  = (2) Rowland Pudsey
- **Daughter (?)** = member of Aslaby family
- **Elizabeth** = William Burgh
- **Margery** = Robert Wycliffe
- **Isabel** = Roger Aske

Christopher's second wife was Margaret Wadisley and 6 children are noted by Whitaker (15).

Christopher Conyers
+ Margaret Wadisley

- **Margaret**
  = Henry Pudsey of Bolton, Yorks.
- **Alice**
  = Henry Wharton
  (Tonge (34) indicates Sir John, below, is her father)
- **Brian** of Pinchinthorpe
  = Elizabeth Nelson
- **Nicholas** of Stainton
- **Conan**, became a priest
- **Henry** of Holtby
  = Cecily, daughter of John Holtby of Fryton

3. Sir John Conyers

There is a long list of the manors he owned - Hornby Castle, Arrathorne, Langthorne, Appleton, Crakeall, Newton Moorcarr, Little Arrington, Aldwarke, Skelton Castle, Marske, Redcar, Brockton, Girrick, Langburgh, and several in Lincolnshire.

He was a military man, distinguishing himself in the Wars of the Roses, and in 1469 he headed an insurrection against Edward IV at Danesmoor, Edgcote, near Banbury. The Battle of Edgcote resulted from dissatisfaction among Yorkshire Lords about high taxes and annual rents instigated by the accomplices of King Edward IV and his Queen, Elizabeth Woodville. The rising was undertaken principally in the interests of a Nevill family coterie involving Richard, Earl of Warwick, George, Archbishop of York, and the King's brother George, Duke of Clarence, aimed not directly at the King but at his powerful henchmen. In order to gain popular support, the northern landowners assumed the pseudonym of a heroic mythical champion, and who better than Robin Hood?

Thus the captain of the Yorkshire objectors bore the name Robin of Redesdale, but he was none other than our own Sir John Conyers; another legend to add to that of his dragon-slaying ancestor. His brother, Sir William Conyers of Marske, near Richmond, has also been implicated as carrying the Robin of Redesdale banner.

Having defeated the enemy at Edgcote, Sir John ordered the beheading of the Earl of Pembroke and his brother Sir Richard Herbert. Following Edward's victory in Lincolnshire at Lose Coat field, Sir John was granted a pardon and became Sheriff of Yorkshire. In 1471 he was a commander at Barnet, where he fought under the defeated Earl of Warwick, Richard Nevill, now under the Lancastrian banner. King Richard III made him a Knight of the Garter in 1483, and up to the time of his death in 1490 he was one of Henry VII's best-respected knights.

But there was more to his life than fighting, for as previously indicated he married Margerie, daughter of the 6th Lord Darcy de Knayth and Meinill, by whom he had 12 children. This marriage, in1431, represented the first of a line of Conyers heirs at Hornby Castle marrying into the most powerful northern families. Others following were those of Fauconberg, Nevill, Dacre, and Clifford.

N.B. William Fitzwilliam (see opposite) was descended from the 12th Century family who were related to the Wentworths of Wentworth-Woodhouse. The arms of Fitzwilliam and Conyers form a heraldic roundel in a window in the Church at Arksey, South Yorkshire. (Plate 7).

The will of William Fitzwilliam dictates that he should be buried in the choir at Sprotborough, and William Conyers was to be an executor of the will.

John Conyers (d.1490)
+ Margerie Darcy (1418-1469)

- **SIR JOHN CONYERS** of Hornby (1st son)
  = Alice Nevill
- **Richard** of Horden (2nd son)
  = Elizabeth Claxton, daughter and co-heir of Robert Claxton, Lord of Horden
- **Christopher** of Hetham (3rd son)
  = Joan Montford
- **Henry**
- **Philip**
- **William**
  = Elizabeth Wadisley
- **Robert**
- **Margery**
  = Rowland Playce
- **Joane**
- **Eleanor**
  = Thomas Markenfield
- **Elizabeth**
  = William Fitzwilliam of Sprotborough
  (see note above)
- **Margaret**
  = Richard Askew

4. Sir John Conyers

This next John, son of John, was killed at Edgcote "in his stirrups" in 1469 at the same Roses Battle in which his father was victorious. By 1463 he had married Alice Nevill who was the daughter and co-heir of William Nevill, Lord Fauconberg and Earl of Kent.

This introduces the Fauconberg connection which is best explained by the pedigree overleaf:-

Barony of Fauconberg 1295

Walter de Fauconberg of Ryse, Holderness
1st Lord Fauconberg in 1295, died 1304
= Agnes de Brus,
daughter of Sir Piers de Brus of Skelton Castle, Cleveland, and Hawise, co-heir of her bother Sir William de Lancaster, Lord of Kendal

Walter, 2nd Lord Fauconberg, died 1318
= (1) Isabel Roos, *daughter of Robert Lord Roos of Helmsley*
=(2) Alice de Killingholm, *of Boythorpe*

Walter slain 1314 at Bannockburn = Anastase, *daughter of Ralph Nevill of Raby*

John (1290-1349) 3rd Lord Fauconberg = Eve, *daughter of Ralph Lord Bulmer of Wilton*

Walter (1319-1362) 4th Lord Fauconberg
=(1) Maud, *sister and co-heir of Sir Wm. de Patteshulle*
= (2) Isabel de Burton

Thomas, 5th Lord Fauconberg of Skelton(1345 - 1407)
= (1) Constance de Felton (d.1402)
= (2) Joan Bromflete, *daughter of Sir Thomas Bromflete*

Spent much time in custody due to his support of the King's French enemies. On 17 August 1403, because of his alleged unsound mind, the brothers Robert and John Conyers were given custody of Skelton Castle and his manors and lands (ref.19 under Fauconberg).It seems that the brothers would be Robert of Ormesby (d.1432) and John of Hornby (d.1413).

John Fauconberg *beheaded at Durham 1405* = Joan Conyers
Daughter of Sir Robert Conyers of Ormesby She later married Sir Thomas Bromflete, son of the below-mentioned Thomas.

John of Gaunt, Duke of Lancaster
Joan de Beaufort (1340-1399)
= Ralph Nevill, 1st Earl of Westmorland

Joan, Baroness Fauconberg (1406 - 1490)
Described in The Complete Peerage as a "fool and idiot from birth."
= William Nevill,
Lord Fauconberg, 8th son, d.1462/3
Took livery in 1422 of all the castles and manors of Thomas Fauconberg. Commanded the vanguard of the Yorkshire Army at Northampton in 1460 and at Towton in 1461. In November 1461 he was made Earl of Kent. The barony of Fauconberg fell into abeyance between their daughters Elizabeth and Alice.

Alice = John Conyers *slain Edgcote 1469*
William, Lord Conyers

Elizabeth = Sir Richard Strangways
Sir James Strangways

Joan = Sir Edward Bethom

The Baroness Fauconberg (Countess of Kent) died in 1490, and in 1491 her estates were shared between her grandsons Sir James Strangways and William, 1st. Lord Conyers, eventually devolving with the latter. The Barony of Fauconberg lay in abeyance until 1903 when it was restored to Marcia Amelia Mary Lane-Fox, 13th Baroness Conyers.

John Conyers' family is outlined below:

John Conyers (d.1469)
+ Alice Nevill (b.1437)

- **WILLIAM, 1st Lord Conyers**
  = (1) Mary Scrope
  = (2) Anne Nevill
- **John**, elder brother of William, but died young. (c.1472)
- **Margery**
  = Sir William Bulmer
- **Anne**
  = Richard, Lord Lumley,
  son of Thomas and Elizabeth, illegitimate daughter of Edward IV.

N.B. Dugdale indicates another son, Reginald Conyers, the progenitor of the Wakerley, Northamptonshire branch.(20).

5. William Conyers, 1st Lord Conyers (1468-1524)

Being less than 2 years of age at the time of his father's death, he did not succeed to the Hornby estate until the death of his grandfather some 20 years later.

He was knighted in 1497, and though he was known as Lord Conyers from 1506-1507, it was not until 17th October 1509 that Henry VIII summoned him to Parliament and he officially became Baron or Lord Conyers. In the same year he had become Bailiff of the Liberty of Richmond, and Constable of Richmond Castle. Additionally, he was Constable of Middleham Castle.

His military exploits saw him serving at the siege of Norham Castle. In 1513 he fought against the Scots at the Battle of Flodden, and he served in Scotland in 1522 under George Talbot, Earl of Shrewsbury.

His ownership of lands was extensive; in addition to his northern and north-eastern manors, he owned the manor of Hardwick and other north Nottinghamshire lands in Kirkby, Woodhouse and Ashfield (49).

Back at Hornby Castle (Pl.5), William considerably rebuilt and extended the building and estate, parts of which are still entire. The entrance archway in the South front is his work as, most probably, is the adjacent keep.

The park at Hornby is said to cover about 700 acres and would have been made by William, though much later in the 1760's it was redeveloped and landscaped for the 8th Lord Conyers (4th Earl of Holderness) by the much-famed designer Lancelot "Capability" Brown.

William provided a bell (since recast twice) for Hornby Church, and in his will of 1494 he directed that the South aisle, built by his great great grandfather, and its Chapel, should be maintained.

He was married twice and had family as follows;-

William, 1st Lord Conyers

= (1) Mary Scrope

= (2) **Anne Nevill**, daughter of Ralph Nevill, 3rd Earl of Westmorland.

- **CHRISTOPHER, 2nd Lord Conyers**
  = Anne Dacre
- **Katherine**
  = Sir Francis Bigod of Settrington
- **Margaret**
  = Sir Richard Cholmley of Rooksby

Mary Scrope was the daughter of John, Lord Scrope of Bolton Castle, Wensleydale. It was planned by a dispensation granted in 1472 that she would marry William's elder brother John, but he died prior to the event. William was not quite aged eleven when the dispensation was granted at York in September 1479 for his marriage to Mary.

The Scrope marriage is indicated childless, though the Beckwith pedigree suggests unconvincingly that it produced the two daughters attributed here to William's father, John. It is certain, however that the male line continued via William's second marriage to Anne Nevill, daughter of Ralph, 3rd Earl of Westmorland. Like his father before him he had married into this great northern dynasty which was established at the Castles of Raby, Middleham, Penrith, Sheriff Hutton, Brancepeth, Snape, and the other Hornby, near Lancaster.

The following chart demonstrates the relationships of the Conyers with the Nevills and the links involving John of Gaunt (Duke of Lancaster), King Richard III and King Edward IV.

Nevill and Conyers Family Links

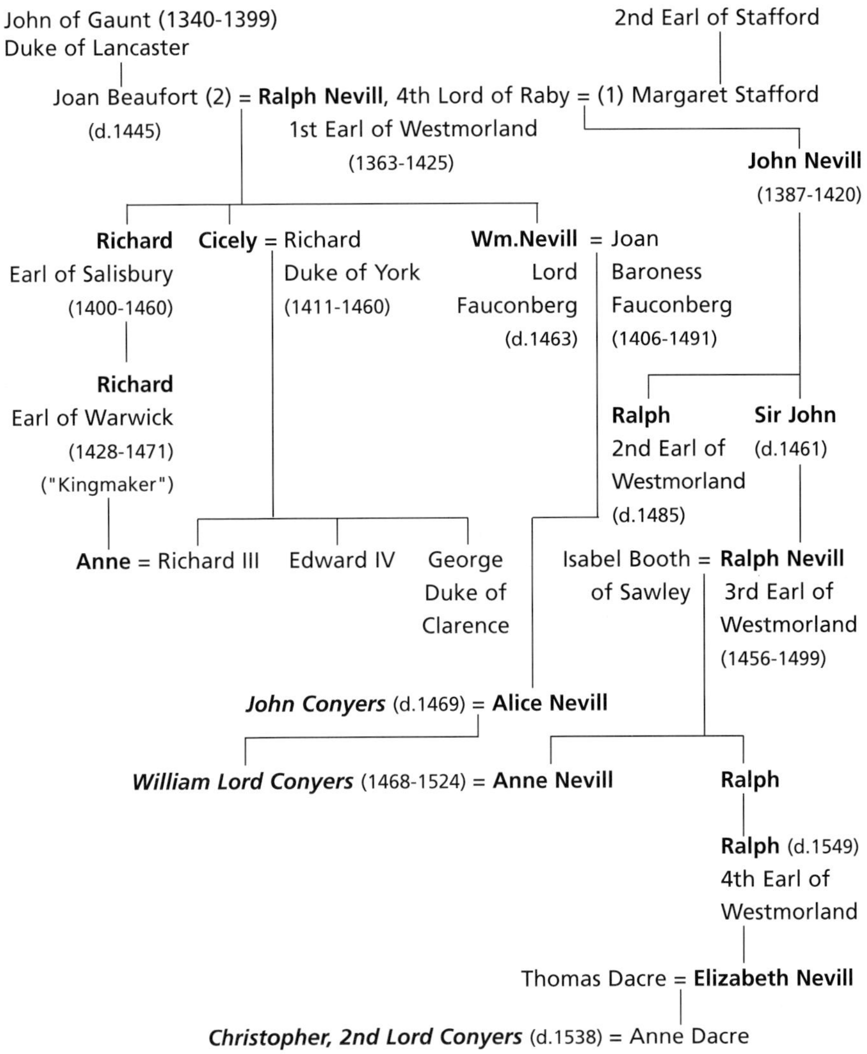

After William's death in 1524 his widow married Anthony Saltmarsh of Hornby in 1525 at Aldwark. His father-in-law, Ralph Nevill, died in 1499 at Hornby Castle, Bedale and is buried in the parish Church there.

6. Christopher Conyers, 2nd Lord Conyers (d.1538)

In 1515 Christopher was married at Kirkoswald to Anne Dacre, daughter of Thomas, Lord Dacre of Gilsland. Thomas was the nephew of Randolf Dacre who was killed in 1461 at the battle of Towton in the Wars of the Roses, and the latter's memorial cross stands on Towton moor.

Christopher was knighted in 1523 and summoned to Parliament by Henry VIII from 1529 to 1536. In 1530/31 he was one of the King's peers who signed the denial of the Pope's supremacy in case of his not consenting to the King's divorce from Catherine of Aragon.

1536 saw the beginning of Robert Aske's rebellion or the Northern Insurrection called The Pilgrimage Of Grace, a protest against religious reforms and the dissolution of the Monasteries. The following year a meeting of the insurgents was called at Pontefract Castle and those present included the Lords Darcy, Scrope, Nevill, Latimer, Lumley, Constable, Conyers, and Norton (who had changed his name from Conyers). The eventual outcome was the execution of most of the participating Northern Lords, also the Abbots at Jervaulx and Fountains Abbeys. Some were hanged at Tyburn, but Lady Bulmer was burned at Smithfield and Sir Thomas Darcy, of whom more shortly, was beheaded on Tower Hill. It appears that Lord Conyers escaped the hangman's noose at this time but he was not to reach longevity as he died the following year in 1538.

His wife is described in her will as Anne, Lady Conyers, Dowager of Skelton, and directs her burial to be "in Skelton, beside my Lord husband."

Hornby Castle, early 19th Century. (Sheffield Libraries and Information)

Their family follows:-

Christopher Conyers, 2nd Lord Conyers (d.1538)
+ Anne Dacre (d.1548)

- **JOHN CONYERS, 3rd Lord Conyers**
  = Maud Clifford, daughter of Henry,
  Earl of Cumberland.
  Lord Bromflete, Vipont and Vesey,
- **Leonard**
  = Alice, daughter of Thomas Laton of Newsham
- **Elizabeth**
  = George Playce of Halnaby, Yorkshire
  (N.B. Beckwith records a second Elizabeth, married to William Brough).
- **Jane**
  = Sir Marmaduke Constable of Everingham, Yorkshire

With the introduction of the Dacre family at this stage it is useful to examine some of the inter-family relationships linking Conyers and Strangways with Darcy, Fauconberg, Bigod and Dacre.

Strangways Connections

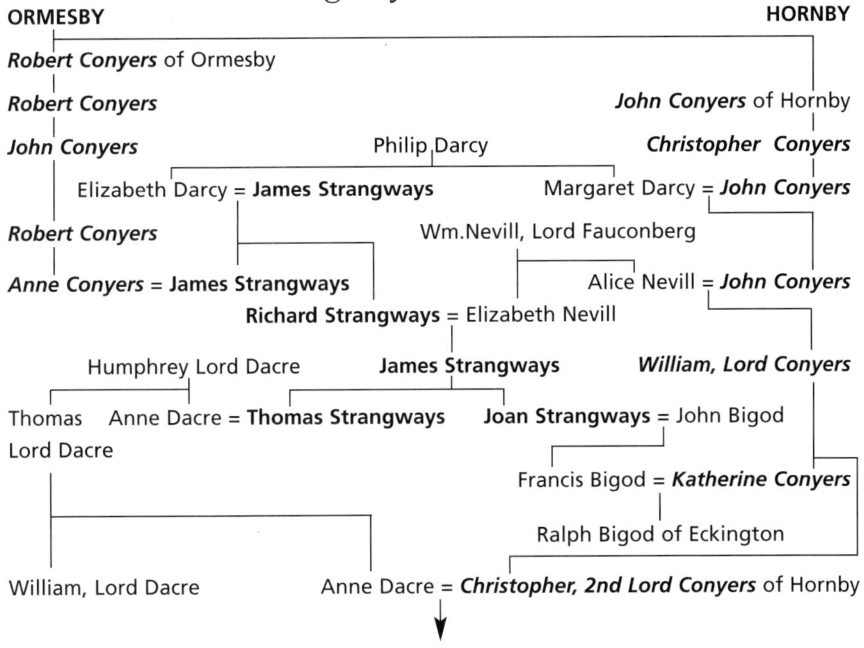

The dates of this small combination of pedigrees range from the deaths of Robert Conyers in 1392 to Christopher, 2nd Lord Conyers, in 1538.

Whilst most of the above relates to events in the North Yorkshire / Cleveland area, it is of interest that in 1340 the North-East Derbyshire manors of Eckington and Mosborough belonged to John, 1st Lord Darcy de Knayth. He was sheriff of the counties of Nottinghamshire, Derbyshire and Lancashire. A visitor to Mosborough Hall today will be able to dine in the John Darcy Restaurant. These manors then passed to Sir James Strangways, an earlier member of the above Strangways family, in 1350. Much later, in 1540, they were owned by William Lord Dacre, brother-in-law of Christopher, 2nd Lord Conyers.

7. John Conyers, 3rd Lord Conyers (1523-1557)

Son and heir of Christopher, John fought alongside the Earl of Hertford at the siege of Leith in 1544 when Leith was taken by the English, and was knighted there.

He was summoned to Parliament from 1544 to 1555. During his time he was Warden of the West Marches and Governor of Carlisle, also Warden of the East Marches and Governor of Berwick. When he was 15 he married Maud Clifford, daughter of the Earl of Cumberland, of Skipton Castle.

Henry Percy, Earl of Northumberland
|
Henry Clifford, 1st Earl of Cumberland = Margaret (2nd wife)
|
Maud = John Conyers

Fig 11

John, 3rd Lord Conyers (Private Collection/Photo courtesy of the National Portrait Gallery, London)

A portrait of John that was at Hornby Castle is described in Whitaker's History of Richmondshire. He is said to be of **"full bluff countenance, expressive at once of good cheer and authority, and very characteristic of the style of Henry VIII."**

John's marriage produced two sons and four daughters, as represented in the chart adjacent.

This demonstrates that when John, 3rd Lord Conyers died in 1557, the Barony fell into abeyance between his three surviving daughters. In1644 his grandson, Conyers Darcy, became the sole representative of the Barony on

John, 3rd Lord Conyers + **Maud Clifford**

- **John**, died without issue
- **Henry**, died without issue
- 1. **Anne** (d.1567) = Sir Anthony Kemp of Slindon, Sussex
  - Henry, died without issue
- 2. **Elizabeth** (1546-1572) = Thomas Darcy (2nd son, d.1605), son of Sir Arthur Darcy
  - ***Conyers Darcy, 4th Lord Conyers***
- 3. **Katherine** (d.1622)
  = (1) Francis Saville of Lupset, Yorkshire
  = (2) John Atherton, of Fryton, Yorks and Atherton, Lancs.
  - John Atherton = Anne, daughter of Sir John Byron
    - Anne (d.1644) = Sir William Pennyman (1607-1643)
- 4. Margaret. Died unmarried

the death of Anne Pennyman who was buried at Oxford with her husband. He also now owned the whole of the Hornby manor. Elizabeth, (John's second daughter) and Thomas Darcy also had a daughter, baptised in 1571. There is a fine monument to Elizabeth in the South Chapel at Hornby Church.

This terminates the Conyers surname in the Barony, by which time the family name had spread to many other parts of the country; Lancashire, Northamptonshire, Essex, and London included.

Their greatest presence was still in the North-East of England, however, and there are other pedigrees showing descents of Conyers at Boulby, Laton, Horden, Marske, Malton, York, Holtby, Hutton Bonville, Whitby, and Scarborough, to name just some (20).

Many of the members of these other branches went on to hold positions of importance and responsibility, for example John Conyers of Horden was created a baronet in 1628 (the baronetcy became extinct in 1810).

A Sir John Conyers was appointed Lieutenant of the Tower of London in 1642, and a Conyers was Lord Mayor of London in 1723. However, these had been better blessed than a Thomas Conyers, the last baronet of Horden, who was a pauper in the workhouse at Chester-le-Street. He inherited from his nephew, Sir George Conyers, the title only, plus the manor of Hutton Bonville (44).

The Darcys

We have previously encountered the Darcy family through the marriage of John Conyers of Hornby (d.1490) to Margerie (or Margaret) Darcy, and of his brother Robert's marriage to Margaret Darcy of Hinton, Lincolnshire. These Darcy daughters, although from the same root, were not immediate relatives.

The Darcy family, as that of Conyers, is of ancient origin, one Norman Darcy being granted 33 lordships in Lincolnshire by the Conqueror. The first Darcy barony was created in 1299 and was held by Sir Philip, Lord Darcy of Nocton and Cawkwell, Lincolnshire. This fell into abeyance in 1350 when the 3rd Baron Darcy died without issue.

In 1332 a further Darcy barony was created, belonging to John, cousin (though some sources say younger brother), of the Philip Darcy of 1299. He held Knayth, Kexby and Upton and to create differentiation the line became known as Lord Darcy de Knayth. The barony of Meinill (sometimes spelt Meynell) became absorbed into the title at an early date and the clearest representation of this link and the connections with the Conyers families can be shown opposite:-

Fig 12

Temple Newsam. A principal home of the Darcys 1337 - 1537

THE DARCYS

Sir Roger Darcy of Oldcotes and Styrrup,
younger brother of Sir Norman Darcy of Nocton

John Lord Darcy 1332

Nicholas de Meinill, Lord Meinill 1336 (d.1341)

John Lord Darcy (d.1356) = Elizabeth (d.1368)

John Lord Darcy (d.1362)

Philip Lord Darcy (d.1399)

John Lord Darcy (d.1411)

Philip Lord Darcy (1398-1418) = Alianor Fitzhugh

Sir John Conyers = **Margaret Darcy**

Sir John Conyers (d.1470)

William, 1st Lord Conyers

Christopher, 2nd Lord Conyers

John, 3rd Lord Conyers

John Darcy, 2nd son, (d.1458)

Richard Darcy

Sir William Darcy (d.1488)

Sir Thomas Darcy, Lord Darcy of Darcy 1509
(beheaded and attainted 1537)

Arthur Darcy
(2nd son, d.1561)

George Darcy (1st son)
(restored to Lord Darcy 1548, d.1558)
= Dorothy Melton of Aston

Elizabeth = **Thomas Darcy**
(d.1572) (d.1605)

Conyers Darcy
4th Lord Conyers (1570-1654)

Conyers Darcy
5th Lord Conyers (1598-1689)
(1st Earl of Holderness)

Conyers Darcy, 6th Lord Conyers (1622-1692)
(2nd Earl of Holderness)

John Darcy, (1659-1689)

Robert Darcy, 7th Lord Conyers (1681-1722)
(3rd Earl of Holderness)

Robert Darcy, 8th Lord Conyers (1718-1788)
(4th Earl of Holderness)

Amelia Darcy, 9th Baroness Conyers (1754-1784)

John 2nd Lord Darcy of Aston
(d.1602)

Michael Darcy
(d.1588)

John 3rd Lord Darcy of Aston
(d.1635)

The principal residence of the Darcy family from 1337 up to the time of the execution of Thomas Darcy in1537 had been Temple Newsam, near Leeds (Fig.12). The house had been previously owned by the Knights Templar, but some time after its confiscation by Henry VIII it passed to the Ingram family who rebuilt parts in the 1620s. The Darcys also owned Temple Hirst, near Selby.

The pedigree shows that Philip, 6th Lord Darcy de Knayth died in 1418 and the barony passed into abeyance between his daughters Elizabeth and Margaret, it subsequently devolving with the latter. This Darcy barony was retored to Conyers Darcy in 1641.

A further Darcy barony called Lord Darcy of Darcy was granted to Sir Thomas Darcy in 1509. He lost this honour, along with his head, when he was executed in 1537 as a result of his part in the Pilgrimage of Grace. In 1548 this barony was restored to his son George, who was then at Aston, so he became known as Lord Darcy of Aston. The pedigree above shows his elder son to be the first Aston (South Yorkshire) connection, and his younger son to be the father of Thomas who married Elizabeth, the 3rd Lord Conyers' heiress.

The Darcys of Aston to 1635

The previous Darcy descent table makes reference to the Darcys of Aston, South Yorkshire, and they are briefly discussed here.

In the 14th Century the manor of Aston passed to William Melton, Archbishop of York 1317-1340, whose niece had married Robert Conyers, father (33,34) or grandfather (35) of John, the Hornby Castle ancestor.

Six Melton generations later, in 1547, Dorothy Melton, daughter of Sir John and Catherine Hastings married George Darcy, son of Sir Thomas Darcy. The lands he acquired were substantial and included the larger of the two manors of Wales, near Sheffield, as well as Aston. The pedigree shows the Melton - Darcy marriage and its subsequent descent to 1635, when on the death of John Lord Darcy, the Barony of Darcy of Aston became extinct. Full accounts of the Aston Darcys prior to Conyers involvement can be found in the publications of Joseph Hunter (18), Philip Barnes (21), and the Aston History Group (22).

Prior to the Aston estates passing to Conyers Darcy in 1680, the Aston pedigree is summarised as shown.

John, 3rd Lord Darcy of Aston, therefore survived his three children, who all died unmarried. It can be seen that 1624 was not a good year for him, losing his only son,

Thomas Darcy (executed 1537) = Dousabel, dau. of Sir Richard Tempest

- 1. **George Darcy** (d.1558) = Dorothy (1505-1557), dau. of Sir John Melton of Aston
  - 2. **John** (1536-1602) = Agnes Babbington of Dethick
    - **Michael** (d.1588) = Margaret, dau. of Thomas Wentworth of Wentworth Woodhouse
      - **Anne** = Henry Savile of Copley
      - **Margaret**
      - 3. **Sir John** (1579-1635) = (1) Rosamund (1576-1607), dau. of Peter, Lord Freschville of Staveley, Derbyshire
        - = (2) Isabel (d.1622), dau. of Sir Christopher Wray, widow of Godfrey Foljambe of Walton, Chesterfield
        - = (3) Mary Bellasis (1605-1624), dau. of Thomas, Lord Fauconberg, sister of Lady Osborne of Kiveton.
        - = (4) Elizabeth, (d.1669), dau. of William West of Firbeck. Her second husband was Sir Francis Fane (1611-1680)
        - **John** (1602-1624)
        - **Rosamund** (d.before 1635)
        - **Elizabeth** (1607-1624)
  - **George**
  - **Clara**
  - **Elizabeth** = Brian Stapleton of Carleton
  - **Mary** = (1) Henry Babbington = (2) Henry Foljambe
  - **Agnes** = Sir William Fairfax of Gilling
  - **Edith** = Sir Thomas Dawney of Cowick
  - **Dorothy** = Sir Thomas Metham
- **Sir Arthur** = Mary Carew
  - **Thomas** = Elizabeth Conyers →

a daughter, and his third wife.
He was known as the "Good Lord Darcy" on account of his generous nature and pious ways.

Of potential confusion is the reference to John's third wife (they were married at Harthill, Yorkshire) being the daughter of Lord Fauconberg. This barony is of Newborough, (or Newburgh), Yorkshire and is not related to the barony of Fauconberg described in an earlier chapter associated with the Nevills and the Conyers.

The above Lord Darcys of Aston lived there on the same site as the current Aston Hall. Sir John's fourth wife Elizabeth continued to live at Aston and own the estate, until her death in1669, as did her second husband Sir Francis Fane till his death in 1680. The inheritance of the estates at Aston then followed the male line of Darcy, not the issue of Anne Darcy and Henry Savile. Thus they passed to Conyers Darcy of Hornby Castle (5th Lord Conyers), in 1680, when he would have been around 82.

Conyers Darcy, 4th Lord Conyers (1570-1654)

Conyers Darcy (Pl.3) was born and baptised at York in 1570. His parents lived at Hornby Castle, inherited by his father Thomas as a result of his marriage to Elizabeth Conyers. After her death, Thomas fathered at least another 15 children by two more wives.

Conyers Darcy attended Caius College, Cambridge when 17, and was knighted by James I in1603. He lived at Hornby and in 1594 married Dorothy Bellasis, daughter of Sir Henry Bellasis of Newborough, Yorkshire, and Ursula, daughter of Sir Thomas Fairfax of Denton, Yorkshire. Dorothy was the aunt to Mary Bellasis who was John Lord Darcy of Aston's third wife. Their family of 7 sons and 9 daughters is summarised below:-

Conyers Darcy + Dorothy Bellasis

- **CONYERS DARCY, 5th Lord Conyers** (1598-1689)
  = Grace Rokeby of Skiers (d.1658)
- **Sir William Darcy** of Wilton Castle
  = Dorothy, dau. of George Selby of Newcastle
- **Henry Darcy** of New Parke and Colburn Hall
  = Mary, daughter of William Scrope of Highley
- **Thomas Darcy** of Winkburn
- **Marmaduke Darcy**, usher to Charles II (d.1681-buried at Windsor)
- **James Darcy** of Sedbury Park, M.P. for Richmond 1660
  = Isabel Wyville *(their son, also James, was created Lord Darcy of Navan, Co. Meath, in 1721)*
- **Edward Darcy**
- **Barbara** = Matthew Hutton of Marske, Yorkshire
- **Ursula** = John Stillington of Kelfield, Yorkshire
- **Margaret** = Sir Thomas Harrison of Allerthorpe
- **Dorothy** = John Dalton of Hawkeswell, Yorkshire
- **Anne** = Thomas Metcalfe of Routh Park, Lincolnshire
- **Grace** = (1) George Best of Middleton
  = (2) Sir Francis Molineux of Mansfield
- **Mary** = Acton Burnell of Winkburn Hall, Nottinghamshire
- **Isabell**
- **Fillydelpha**

When Philip, 6th Lord Darcy de Knayth died in 1418, this barony went into abeyance between his two daughters, Margaret (who married Sir John Conyers), and Elizabeth (who married Sir James Strangways). With the subsequent failure of the Strangways line and the extinction of the Darcy of Aston branch, the Darcy barony became restored to Conyers Darcy in 1641. So did the barony of Conyers, but not without the complications that can sometimes confuse these peerages. In the Parliament which first met at Westminster in November 1640 he petitioned Charles I for the restoration to him of the title Baron Darcy. Early the following year a Royal Warrant directed the preparation of two bills to restore to Conyers Darcy, then in his 71st. year, "the liberties, places and states" of John Lord Darcy and of John Lord Conyers. These two Letters Patent stated that (1) Conyers Darcy should be Lord Darcy and (2) Conyers Darcy, Lord Darcy, should be Lord Conyers. Amazingly, these two Letters Patent are lost but the wording of the Warrant seems clearly to seek the restoration of the ancient Darcy de Knayth and Meinill barony of 1332. It would be understandable that Conyers Darcy would prefer the Darcy title owing to its older precedence and his own male descent from its holders. He was summoned to Parliament in October 1641 and took his seat the following January as Lord Darcy and Conyers. He was the first of a line of five to hold what they themselves probably considered to be a joint barony.

The Complete Peerage (19) carries some interesting discussion as to whether there was meant to be a creation of the joint barony Lord Darcy and Conyers, limited to the male line (which would have become extinct in 1778 on the death of the 8th Lord Conyers), or whether the two separate baronies were deemed to be terminations of abeyances. In 1903 the Committee of Privileges decided in favour of the latter. This decision, albeit long after the event, conflicts somewhat with respect to the Conyers barony since in 1641 it was still abeyant with Anne Pennyman, and therefore could not have been terminated at that time. When Anne died in 1644, the Conyers barony in its own right passed to Conyers Darcy.

Both Conyers and his wife died within a year of each other in 1653-1654 and both are buried at Hornby.

Conyers Darcy, 5th Lord Conyers (1598-1689)

He was baptised at Kirkby Fleetham in 1598. In1616 at Wentworth, he married Grace, only daughter and heiress of Thomas Rokeby of Skiers, and Mary, nee Cartwright, of Ossington, Nottinghamshire. Conyers (Pl.3) was Constable of Middleham Castle from 1660 to 1671.

In 1661 he was first summoned to parliament in his late father's barony of Darcy. Later writs of summons in 1678 and 1680 added the words "and Meinill", but any assumption to the title of Meinill was without any legal foundation. He inherited the estates at Aston in 1680, and was created Earl of Holderness in 1682. This Earldom followed directly from the day of the burial of the previous Earl, Prince Rupert, Duke of Bavaria, but they were not in the slightest degree connected. In 1689 he sold Skiers to Sir William Rokeby, so it was back in the Rokeby family once more. His wife Grace died in 1658 but Conyers reached the ripe old age, especially for those days, of 91 before he died at Hornby, where he and his wife are buried. The third bell at the Church there had been recast by him in 1656.

Their family of 13, presumably much ravaged by The Black Death, was:-

Conyers Darcy (1598-1689)
+
Grace Rokeby (died 1658)

- **Conyers Darcy, 6th Lord Conyers** (1622-1692) = 4 wives
- **John Darcy**, buried at Hornby in 1618
- **John Darcy** (1619-1621). Buried at Hornby
- **Rokeby**
- **Philip**, baptised and buried at Hornby in 1626
- **Jo....** , baptised and buried at Hornby in 1630
- **Ursula** = Sir Christopher Wyville of Burton Constable, Yorkshire
- **Grace** = Sir John Ligard of Ganton, Yorkshire
- **Margaret** = Sir Henry Marwood of Little Buskby, Yorkshire
- **Elizabeth** = Sir Henry Stapleton of Myton, Yorkshire
- **Anne**, died unmarried
- **Mary**, died young
- **Dorothy**, died young

Conyers Darcy, 6th Lord Conyers (1622-1692)

This third successive Conyers Darcy was baptised at St. Michael le Belfrey, York, and educated at University College, Oxford. Taking up law, he was admitted to Gray's Inn in 1640.

He became M.P. for Boroughbridge in 1660 and M.P. for Yorkshire from 1661 to 1679. He was an ardent Royalist in the Civil War, and was Captain in Prince Rupert's Horse in 1667. In 1671 he succeeded his father as Constable of Middleham Castle. The year 1680 saw him summoned to the House of Lords, this time in his father's barony of Conyers, but he was usually styled Lord Darcy and Conyers. Parochial papers of Aston church confirm that he signed himself as "Darcy and Conyers". He married four times:-

1. In 1645 at Mereworth, Kent, to Catherine Fane (d.1649), daughter of Francis Fane, Earl of Westmorland, and Mary Mildmay. Catherine was the sister of Sir Francis Fane of Aston who married Elizabeth West, widow and fourth wife of John, Lord Darcy of Aston.

2. In 1650 at Clerkenwell to Frances Howard (1628-1670). She was the daughter of Thomas Howard, Earl of Berkshire, and Elizabeth Cecil (daughter of Wiiliam Cecil, Earl of Exeter). Frances died at Hornby and was buried there.

3. In1676 to Frances Seymour (d.1681), widow of the Earl of Southampton. She was the daughter of William Seymour, 2nd Duke of Somerset, and Frances Devereux (daughter of Robert Devereux, 2nd Earl of Essex). Frances was buried at Westminster Abbey.

4. In1685 to Elizabeth Freschville (1635-1690), widow of Philip Warwick, and daughter of John, Lord Freschville of Staveley, Derbyshire. She was the niece of Rosamund Freschville, the first of John, Lord Darcy of Aston's four wives.

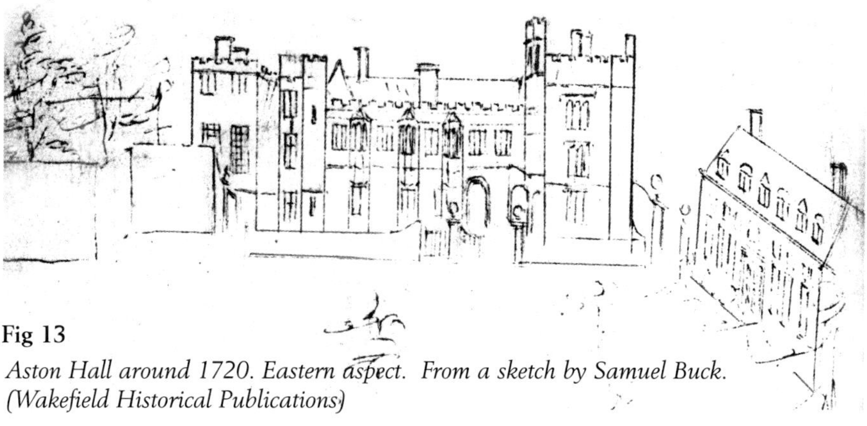

Fig 13

Aston Hall around 1720. Eastern aspect. From a sketch by Samuel Buck. (Wakefield Historical Publications)

On the death of Sir Francis Fane in 1680, Aston Hall (Fig.13) would have become vacant and it is likely that Conyers lived there during the latter years of his life, particularly since his fourth wife was of local stock. He was a great benefactor to Aston church, providing many valuable material gifts, including a silver chalice with patten. Other gifts donated by him and his third wife, the Countess of Southampton, in 1677, included a rich satin cloth and gold-embroidered cushion for the pulpit, a cloth and cushion for the communion table, and two prayer books. A great iron-bound chest and black hearse-cloth figure among the more unusual, yet practical donations. There was also a financial provision for annual distribution to the poor.

Conyers died at Aston in 1692 having held the title Earl of Holderness for just the three years since his father's death in 1689. He was buried at Hornby, and his wife, who had died two years earlier, was buried at Staveley. He had therefore outlived all his four wives.

Conyers Darcy's offspring were by his second wife Frances Howard and are shown below:-

Conyers Darcy (1622-1692)
+
Frances Howard (1628-1670)

- John Darcy (1659-1689) = Bridget, dau. of Robert Sutton, Lord Lexington
- Philip Darcy (1661-1715) M.P. for Richmond. Died unmarried
- Charles Darcy (1666-1715) Died unmarried
- Grace (1655-1656)
- Frances (1657-1658)
- Elizabeth

Of great significance is that his son John, who was baptised at Hornby in 1659, participated in the great Revolution Plot of 1688. This changed the face of British history and was a scheme to bring William of Orange over from Holland to replace King James II, but fundamentally to preserve the Protestant faith as opposed to James II's avowed Catholicism. It is usually reported that there were four ringleaders in the plot; John Darcy, the Earl of Devonshire, (later to become the first Duke of Devonshire), the Earl of Danby, (who later became the first Duke of Leeds) and Lord Delamere (later the Earl of Warrington).

To hatch their plans they met at The Cock and Pynot Inn at Whittington, Chesterfield, now known as Revolution House, and open to the public. The outcome was that William landed in England in November 1688 and James II fled to France. William and his wife Mary, eldest daughter of James II, became King and Queen of England in February 1689.

John Darcy did not live to see the events fully unfold having died of "ye squinsey at London" in January 1689; nor did he become heir apparent to the titles since his death preceded that of his grandfather. He was buried at Westminster Abbey. During his lifetime he had been M.P. for Richmond from 1681 to 1688 and also M.P. for the county of York.

The succession of the baronies of Darcy, Conyers, and the Earldom of Holderness therefore became dependent on the children of John Darcy. He had married Bridget, daughter of Robert Sutton, Lord Lexington, and sole heir of her brother Robert.

They had seven children:-

John Darcy (1659-1689) + Bridget Sutton

- **Robert Darcy**, (1681-1722) **7th Lord Conyers** = Frederica Schomberg (1688-1751) Countess of Mertola (Portugal)
- **Sir Conyers Darcy** (d.1758) = (1) Mary Bentinck, dau. of the Earl of Portland
  = (2) Elizabeth Rotherham of Much Waltham, Essex
  (he was M.P. for York in 1707, Master of the Horse to Queen Anne and George I, subsequently comptroller of the Household and member of the Privy Council)
- **Norman Darcy** (1679-1681) Buried at Hornby
- **John Darcy**, born and died in London in 1683
- **Francis**, born and died at Aston in 1679
- **Elizabeth** (d. 1720) = Sir Ralph Milbanke, of Halnaby, Yorkshire
- **Charlotte** (d. 1760 Gt. Marlborough St.) = Wardel George Westley of Ravenfield, Rotherham

Robert Darcy, 7th Lord Conyers (1681-1722)

Robert was born in London in 1681 but registered at Hornby, later being styled Lord Darcy and Conyers.

In 1692 he succeeded his grandfather as 3rd Earl of Holderness. His positions included Constable of Middleham Castle 1702, Chief Justice in Eyre, North of Trent 1714, Lord Lieutenant of the North Riding 1714-1722, First Lord of Trade and Plantations 1718-1719, and Lord of the Bedchamber to King George I 1719-1722.

He is described by Macky in his publication "Characters", about 1706 as a **"very young gentleman, hath been abroad in the world; a lover of the constitution of his country to a great degree; of good nature, fair complexion, not 30 years old"**.

In 1715 at Hillingdon, Middlesex, he married Frederica, daughter and co-heir of Meinhardt Schomberg, 3rd Duke of Schomberg and Duke of Leinster. Frederica owned the title of Countess of Mertola (Portugal).

Links with the Revolution were maintained, since her grandfather, Frederick Hermon Schomberg, joined up with William, Prince of Orange's expedition in 1688. It was Schomberg who, with a force ten thousand strong, started the Irish campaign at Carrickfergus Castle in 1689.

Robert Darcy died at Bath in 1722, aged 40, and was buried at Hornby. His widow, who was born in Berlin, remarried in 1724 with Benjamin Mildmay, Earl Fitzwalter. She died in 1751, aged 63 and was buried at Chelmsford, Essex.

It seems reasonable to assume that Aston Hall was well utilised in these times. Certainly Robert's brother Sir Conyers Darcy stayed there as Hunter records joyous Christmas-time festivities when Sir Conyers continued dancing despite having just been told that one wing of the mansion was on fire (18). Apparently this fire virtually destroyed the house and was one of several fires over the years, but this was the most serious. The party in question, seemingly in the 1730s, was open to the general public, and the seat of the fire was in a remote and little used wing. The net result, following yet another fire in 1767, was that a new hall was eventually built in 1772 for Robert's son, also Robert, who became 4th Earl of Holderness, 8th Lord Conyers. Pieces of armorial stained glass from the old Hall bearing Darcy shields of arms now form the east window of Aston Church. (Fig.42 and Pl. 8).

Hornby Castle was not being neglected, however. In the early 18th Century, Robert had fitted sash windows, and panelling was installed in the dining-room.

Robert and Frederica's family was as follows:-

Robert Darcy (1681-1722) + **Frederica Schomberg (1688-1751)**

- **Robert Darcy** (1718-1778) **8th Lord Conyers**
  = Mary, daughter of Frances Doublet, Member of the States of Holland
- **George Schomberg Darcy**
  (born 1716 at St. James, London; died in infancy)
- **Meinhardt Frederick Darcy**
  (died young)
- **Louisa Caroline (d.1778)**
  = William Henry Kerr, Earl of Ancram, later Marquess of Lothian

Robert, 3rd Earl of Holderness, 7th Lord Conyers (In a private Scottish Collection)

Robert Darcy 8th Lord Conyers (1718-1778)

Robert was baptised at St Martin-in-the-Fields, London, and became 4th and last Earl of Holderness, inheriting the title before he was four years old.

His early education was undertaken by his uncle, Sir Conyers Darcy, who lived sometimes at Aston Hall, and who would have given him an early upbringing into the ways of public service. Sir Conyers was a wealthy courtier who also owned Aske Hall (Richmond, Yorkshire), and property in Richmond and London. Robert was styled Lord Darcy and Conyers, being educated at Westminster School and Trinity College, Cambridge, though it does not appear that he ever took his degree.

He was made Constable of Middleham Castle in 1739 and held many political posts. In 1740 he was appointed Lord Lieutenant of the North Riding of Yorkshire, a position he held until 1777. In 1741 he became one of the Lords of the King's Bedchamber, and in that capacity attended George II to Hanover in 1743, being present with him at the Battle of Dettingen that year.

May 1744 saw Robert appointed Ambassador to Venice, where he lived for two years prior to returning to England in the autumn of 1746. In May 1749 he became Minister to The

Hague for two years before returning to England yet again. On 21st June 1751, in Henry Pelham's Ministry, he was appointed Secretary of State for the South, and on the same day was sworn of the Privy Council. He transferred to the position of Secretary of State for the North from 1754 to 1761. During George II's absence from England from 1752 to 1755, he had been one of the Lord Justices of the Realm. In 1761 he was Cupbearer to the Queen Consort at the Coronation of George III, yet was dismissed from office the same year, being replaced by Lord Bute. William Pitt, the other Secretary of State, was dismissed about the same time, the King saying **"I had two Secretaries, one of whom could do nothing, the other would do nothing ...".**

Robert, or Holderness as he was known, was consoled for his loss of office with an annual pension of £4000, and in 1765 until his death, with the reversion of the Wardenship of the Cinque Ports. In April 1771 to 1776 he was Governor of the Prince of Wales, later George IV, and of his brother Prince Frederick, later Duke of York. George III had invited the somewhat reluctant Holderness to be their Governor, and the boys, aged around 8 and 9, led him a merry dance, despite all his conscientiousness, moral sentiment, and good advice. In 1774, Robert's health suffered, necessitating a "long stay on the Continent", and he eventually resigned his duties to the young princes in 1776.

Robert was a Whig until 1770, a Tory thereafter though he may not have described himself as such, and may have owed his political position more to his rank and foreign connections than to his intellectual qualities. Horace Walpole had alluded to him as **"an unthinking and unparliamentary minister"**, **"a baby politician"**, and **"that formal piece of dullness"**. Yet he was not as incapable as Walpole would have us believe. The Duke of Newcastle succeeded in making him a Secretary of State when only thirty-three, and in a letter to his brother, Henry Pelham, Robert is described thus:- **"He is indeed, or was, thought trifling in his manner and carriage: but, believe me, he has a solid understanding, and will come out as prudent a young man as any in the kingdom. He is good-natured, so you may tell him his faults, and he will mend them. He is universally loved and esteemed, almost by all parties, in Holland. He is very taciturn, dexterous enough, and most punctual in the execution of orders. He is got into the routine of business. He knows very well the present state of it. He is very diligent and exact in all his proceedings. He has great temper, mixed with proper resolution. He has no pride about him, though a D'Arcy."**

He may not have taken much part in House of Lords debates and few of his speeches are reported.

In the earlier part of his life Robert had a great passion for directing operas, and in 1743 the London opera was under the sole management of himself and Lord Middlesex. This explains the following epigram, made on his appointment as Secretary of State:-

**"That secrecy will not prevail in politics is certain
Since Holderness, who gets the seals, was bred behind the curtain"**

In addition to his love of opera, Robert was an important member of the Dilettanti Society. Their art collection has an interesting and unusual portrait of him as a young man. He is shown as a gondolier on Venice's Grand Canal. (Fig 15)

Fig 15

Robert, 4th Earl of Holderness, 8th Lord Conyers, aged around 31.
(Society of Dilettanti and Courtauld Institute of Art)

Following his dismissal from Office, with the significant income from his pensions, he started on improvements to his estates, though he sold Aske Hall, near Richmond, in 1763. Robert hired the famous Venetian architect Giacomo Leonii, to work on his London house, 4, Whitehall Yard, while James Stuart designed a new London house called Holderness House about 1760-1765. Additionally, he is said to have rebuilt Sion Hill House near Isleworth, Middlesex, which he had bought in 1755. This latter property was later occupied by George, fourth Duke of Marlborough, but it no longer exists. Holderness House, off Park Lane, was purchased in 1822 by Charles William Vane (formerly Stewart), 3rd Marquess of Londonderry.

Work at Hornby Castle commenced probably in the late 1750's - early 1760's and mainly involved the rebuilding of the South and East ranges between the medieval towers, the main architect here being John Carr of York, for whom it would have been one of his earlier projects.

Externally, both at Hornby and Sion Hill, 'Capability' Brown, the greatest practitioner of the day, was called in to re-landscape the grounds and parks. At Hornby, the medieval deer park was enclosed, three linked lakes were constructed and three eye-catching model farms were erected. The latter were likely to have been

Robert Darcy, 4th Earl of Holderness, 8th Lord Conyers. (Courtesy of Lady Diana Miller)

designed by Carr, and were called Arbour Hill, (Plate 4), Home Farm and Street Farm. The Hornby estate would have become something of a showpiece, much enhanced by Robert's knowledge of agriculture and crop husbandry.

Back at Aston, following the fire about 1767, John Carr designed a new Hall on the same site as the old one. This was completed in 1772, (Plate 3), although by this time the family were back at Hornby Castle, reportedly having been there by September 1770. A letter around 1773 from Robert's good friend at Aston, Rev. Wiiliam Mason, to Horace Walpole, suggested that Robert may have preferred Hornby because Aston was considered too close to the Duke of Leeds' seat at Kiveton. The two locations are in fact barely two miles apart, visible to each other across the fields.

William Mason had been installed in Aston rectory by Robert, and being a poet, he addressed a sonnet to him expressing his thanks for his friendship and generosity. The poem appeared in Mason's publication "Poems" in 1764, but their friendship later declined as a result of a quarrel.

Robert's estate in South Yorkshire alone was considerable, occupying large areas in the Aston, Aughton, Hardwick, Todwick and Wales districts. Adjacent to the east was the estate of Thomas Osborne, 4th Duke of Leeds. The Holderness estate is shown in detail and in colour on an enormous map approximately 9 ft. by 9 ft. which he commissioned in 1762. This map, discovered in a Rotherham refuse skip in 1988, is in a good state of preservation. It was sold at auction in April 1999. (Plate 3)

It is unlikely that Robert ever lived in his new house at Aston, and not long after its completion the Hall was sold to Harry Verelst who had succeeded Clive of India as Governor of Bengal. It remained in the Verelst family until 1918, and let by them for a time afterwards. The estate was sold in lots in 1928 and the Hall purchased by Ronald Matthews, later knighted. He was chairman of the old London and North-Eastern Railway. Enthusiasts will recall there was an A4 class express steam locomotive named after him. The Hall was later converted into a mental home and subsequently into the pleasant country-house hotel which is now its function.

In November 1742 at The Hague, Robert Darcy married Mary, daughter of Francis Doublet of Groeneveldt, Member of the States of Holland, and they had family as follows:-

Robert Darcy (1718-1778) + **Mary Doublet** (1721-1801)

- **George** (1745-1747)
- **Thomas** (born and died in 1750)
- **Amelia, 9th Baroness Conyers** (1754-1784)
  = (1) Francis Godolphin Osborne
  = (2) John Byron

The Earldom of Holderness became extinct on Robert's death in 1778 at Sion Hill, Middlesex. His widow died at Holderness House, Hertford Street, Mayfair in 1801 aged 80, and they were both buried at Hornby. Mary had donated the Church's font in 1783 and there is a marble memorial to Robert in the north aisle.

His portrait, painted by George Knapton in 1752, is exhibited at Temple Newsam, near Leeds, a former residence of his ancestors (Fig. 16). A copy of Robert's Will of 14th Feb. 1778 forms part of the Duke of Leeds' collection at The Yorkshire Archaeological Society, and this shows that Sion Hill and Holderness House were left firstly to his wife, whilst Amelia, his only surviving child, inherited his other estates. Furniture, books, pictures and stock at Hornby were specifically bequeathed to his son-in-law, the Marquis of Carmarthen at that time, and £5000 was left to his sister Louisa Caroline, the Marchioness of Lothian.

With there being no surviving male heir, Amelia therefore became Baroness Conyers.

Amelia Darcy
9th Baroness Conyers
(1754-1784)

Born in London in 1754, she was baptised at St. George's, Hanover Square, and was married there in 1773 to Francis Godolphin Osborne, Marquess of Carmarthen.

He was then aged 22, afterwards in 1789 becoming 5th Duke of Leeds. On her father's death in 1778, Amelia (Lady Carmarthen) inherited the Conyers Barony as well as Hornby Castle. The 1903 Committee of Privileges decision also determined that the Barony of Darcy could pass down the female line, so posthumously she was also 12th Baroness Darcy (de Knayth). She also carried the title Countess of Mertola (Portugal), originally that of her grandmother.

Just 7 months after her father's death, Amelia, then 24, eloped with Captain John Byron, son of Admiral John Byron, and following her divorce, married him in June 1779 at St.George's, Hanover Square. This was a fashionable place for weddings, Shelley, Disraeli, George Eliot, and the 12th Lord Conyers all having tied the knot there. (Fig.18).

Fig 17

Amelia, 9th Baroness Conyers (Courtesy of Lady Diana Miller)

There are various reports describing Amelia's relationship with her husbands, which would seem to be based on whether the reporter's allegiance lay with Osborne or with Byron. In Sir Herbert Croft's satirical work "The Abbey of Kilkhampton" it is said that she **"dared fly from the arms of a husband who treated her with tenderness to the embraces of a profligate who from a spirit of gallantry consented to a union which neither his honour or his inclination prompted him to accept.**

Forsaken by the man she seduced, despised by the world, and then only compelled to a sense of her misconducts, she fled for refuge to the gloom of retired concealment, where the obloquy of the world disturbed not the tranquillity of her reflections."

Elsewhere in the same work, Amelia's husband (Osborne) is heaped with praise:- **"A nobleman who, in an age of dissipation, preserved his honour and integrity unspotted. His political conduct was ever directed by the principles of virtue, to the detriment of his temporal interests. His domestic tranquillity, though disquieted for a moment by the infidelity of a woman who merited the contempt she ever after experienced, returned to him with new charms in the possession of _ _".** The name is left blank. Maybe it was intended for his second wife, Catherine Anguish.

Whilst accepting that John Byron may have been an incurable romantic and spendthrift, there are also various insights into the character of Francis Osborne, many of them uncomplimentary. Horace Walpole, who never pulled his punches, describes him as a **"light variable young man, of very moderate parts, and less principles".**

An amusing comment on his activities occurs in The Farington Diary 1799. It is said that he constantly attended the Literary Club where he drank three pints of claret nightly, kept late hours till three or four in the morning, gamed, and was fond of low company. The Duke and Duchess were reported as **"on account of his irregular mode of proceeding, not to be very comfortable together".**

The site of his St. James Square house was later to become offices of the Distillers Company.

A characterisation of him that is described as fair was provided by Lord Rosebery:- **"upright and well intentioned, but vain and inadequate."**

A further interesting facet of Francis' character is that he was a lover of cricket, and in his position as Foreign Secretary he arranged a tour of English cricketers to France at the time of the French Revolution. The tour did not take place due to the political situation at that time, and subsequent history has proved that this was just the fore-runner of many similarly aborted tours. (36)

Francis also had a keen interest in dramatic literature, but as he died in 1799 when George Byron was 11, one can only surmise if he would have appreciated the poet's works.

John Byron remarried after Amelia's death, and it was by his second wife that he fathered Lord Byron the poet.

The families can be shown as follows:-

OSBORNE, DARCY AND BYRON LINKS

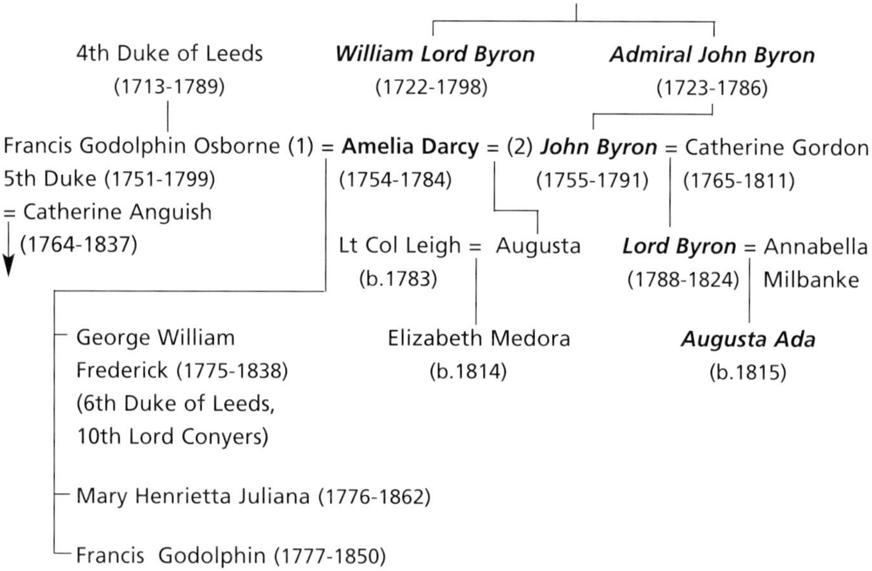

The Byron Connection

The circumstances of Amelia's elopement were such that she formed a relationship with John Byron in 1778 which aroused her husband Francis' suspicions to an extent that on returning to London from the country, he was wont to question the servants about his wife's activities.

Amelia would have none of this, and was carried by sedan to her lovers father's house in Bolton Street, London. She sent her footman to Green Street, Grosvenor Square (where Mrs Byron lived during her husband's absence in the West Indies) to fetch Captain Byron. After a short stay at Bolton Street, they travelled together to Chislehurst, Rottingdean, and other places.

Amelia's trial for adultery resulted in the pronouncement of divorce at Doctors' Commons on 26 March 1779, and on 9 June they were wed at St. George's, Hanover Square.

The Byron connection should be examined in a little more detail, for it would be an understatement to say that the Byrons of this age led very colourful lifestyles.

William, born 1722, was the 5th Baron Byron of Rochdale and his main claim

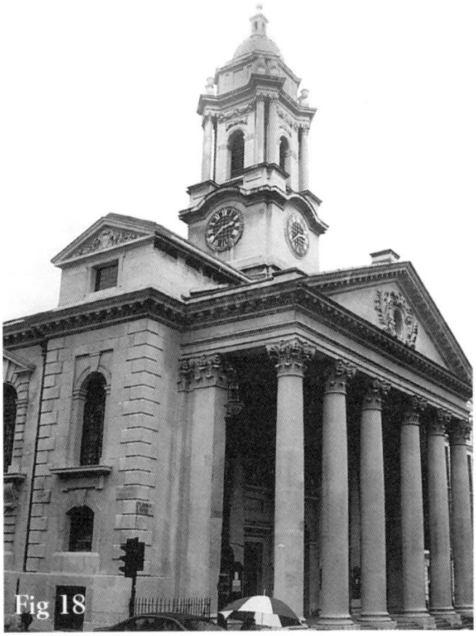

Fig 18

St. George's, Hanover Square, London. Amelia married both her husbands here.

to fame was his killing in a duel in a locked room, not without strong suspicion of foul play, of his relative William Chaworth of Annesley.

He was found guilty of manslaughter but was discharged under the statute of Privilege as a Peer! Being known as the "wicked lord", he sold his property in Rochdale together with the family pictures and partly dismantled the mansion at Newstead. His brother, the Hon. John Byron and Admiral, was so violent and luckless that he was nick-named "Foulweather Jack". Thus, Amelia eloped with John, son of the above John, and in turn he was nick-named "Mad Jack".

"Mad Jack" Byron was an Army person, appointed ensign in the Coldstream Guards in July 1773. He was promoted to Lieutenant and Captain in May 1777, and held the rank of Adjutant from July 1778 to June 1779. He had served in America in 1775 after the outbreak of war there, and it was on his return that his relationship with Amelia was forged. Following their marriage and John's retirement from the Army in 1780, they set up home in Paris, where their three children were born. Their first daughter, Sophia Georgina died young, and their son died soon after birth. The third child, and the sixth that Amelia had produced in eight years (three by her first husband, Francis), was born in 1783 and named Augusta Mary.

Amelia's untimely death in London in January 1784 "of a lingering disorder", probably tuberculosis, was said to have been caused by her accompanying her husband to a hunt too soon after Augusta's birth. She was buried at Hornby, aged just twenty-nine years. Her portrait, by Francois-Hubert Drouais in 1764 when Amelia could have been only ten, is on display, like that of her father, at Temple Newsam. (Fig.17). Both portraits are owned by Lady Diana Miller, daughter of the 14th and last Lord Conyers.

The Captain next turned his attentions to Catherine Gordon of Gight, Aberdeen, marrying her in

London in 1785, yet returning to France to escape his debtors. It was here that Catherine nursed Augusta through a serious illness, but in 1787 she came back to London to prepare for her own confinement, bringing Augusta with her. Shortly afterwards, Augusta was sent to live with Mary, Lady Holderness, her maternal grandmother, to be brought up by "aristocratic relations".

The union of the Captain and Catherine Gordon produced George Gordon in 1788, who became 6th Lord Byron on the death of his great uncle in 1798, the direct line having predeceased him. "Mad Jack" the Captain died of drink in 1791 but not before having squandered the £23,000 Gordon fortune after that of Amelia.

George Lord Byron was renowned for his succession of women as well as his poetry. Possibly one of the reasons he left England for good in 1816 was the gossip surrounding his relationship with his half-sister Augusta in London, and at Newstead Abbey, in 1813/14.

Augusta married her cousin, Colonel George Leigh, in 1807, and it has been widely implicated that she and George Byron had an incestuous affair which may even have produced the child Elizabeth Medora. Such a relationship was never categorically proved and the child was raised normally along with the other six in the Leigh family, Byron never singling her out for any special attention. Yet his poem "Epistle to Augusta" alludes to a relationship much more intense than usual between brother and sister. (38).

In September 1813, Byron came to be staying at Aston Hall as guest of his old Cambridge college friend James Wedderburn Webster and his wife, Lady Frances Annesley. Presumably the Hall was being let at this time, since records show it to be in the ownership of the Verelst family before and after this date. It is ironic, therefore, that Byron should find himself at the location once lived in by his father's first wife, the mother of the woman with whom he was now so involved. Such coincidence was not lost on Byron, as he makes reference to it in a letter to his friend Thomas Moore, though the supposition that his father inherited Aston and resided there is incorrect.

The extent to which Amelia lived at Aston old Hall is not documented but it would seem probable that she would have spent much time at her father's London homes.

Byron's own marriage to Annabella Milbanke took place in 1815 but lasted barely 12 months. (41).

Plate 1

The Conyers Falchion, now displayed at Durham Cathedral. (The Dean and Chapter of Durham)

Below: Sockburn Church

Above: Sockburn Church. Late 13th/early 14th Century effigy of a Conyers, with winged serpent at his feet

Below: Croft-on-Tees bridge, with its 15th Century arches, a venue for the falchion exchange ceremony

Plate 2

Left and below: Hornby Castle. 19thC. water colours

Below left: Parish Church of St. Mary, Hornby, showing the early 15thC. south aisle of John Conyers

Bottom: Hornby Church. Effigy in Derbyshire alabaster, believed to represent John Conyers, d.1412

Plate 3

Above: 8th Lord Conyers' map; the cartouche, entitled 'A plan of the manors of Aston and Wales in the West Riding of the County of York belonging to the Rt. Honourable Robert Earl of Holderness - surveyed by G. Jackson 1762', (Reproduced from the original)

Top Right: Detail of 4th Lord Conyers
Right: 5th Lord Conyers.
(Private Collections/Photos courtesy of the National Portrait Gallery, London)

Below: Aston Hall, built 1772

Plate 4

Right: Kiveton Hall, east aspect

Below: Church of All Hallows, Harthill

Below: Hornby Castle, south front. A gap in the virginia creeper exposes the mid 18th Century Darcy shield

Below: Looking south from Hornby Castle, the telephoto lens picks out Arbour Hill Farm and part of the lakes

Plate 5

Hornby Castle today

Above: south west aspect

Right: south east aspect showing the 15thC. 'keep' tower of William, 1st Lord Conyers

Below: Winter sunshine picks out the eastern outline of Hornby Castle

Plate 6

Above: Shield of arms of the Pelham family on an early monument in Brocklesby Church

Above: Sackville George Pelham, 5th Earl of Yarborough, 14th Lord Conyers (courtesy Lady Wendy Lycett)

Brocklesby Park

Right: Late 1930's (courtesy Lady Wendy Lycett)

Below: Since the 1956-58 rebuild (courtesy Lord Yarborough)

Plate 7

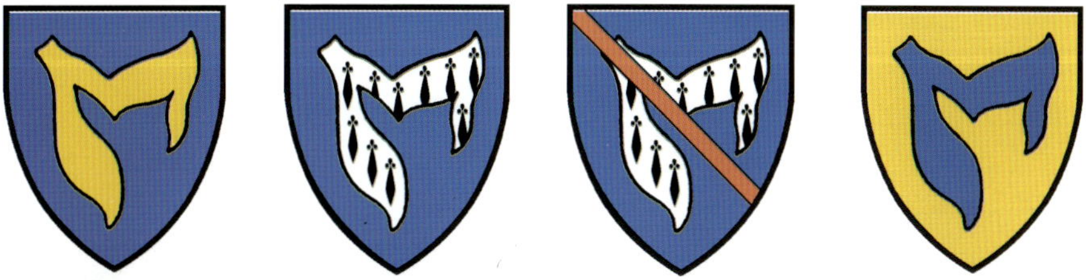

The Shield of arms of Conyers; the maunch or sleeve
Left to right: Sockburn and Hornby, Hutton Conyers, Norton Conyers, Ormesby

Above: The Hornby Portal (Glasgow Museums; The Burrell Collection)

Right: Hypothetical colour representation of the central shields

Left: Arksey Church, roundel of the arms of Fitzwilliam and Conyers

Above right: Harthill Church. Arms of 6th Duke of Leeds, 10th Lord Conyers

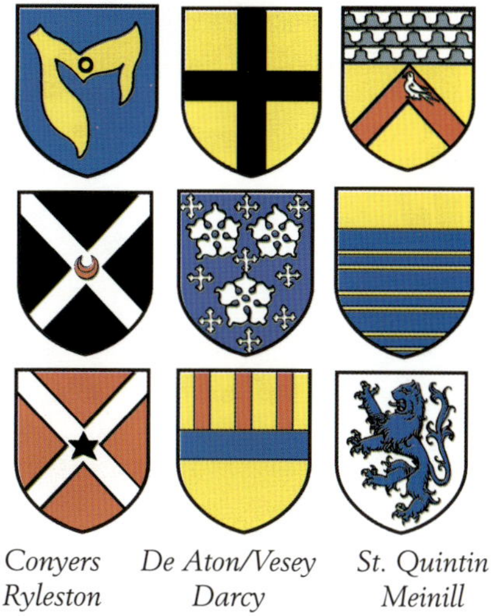

Conyers Ryleston Nevill

De Aton/Vesey Darcy Fauconberg

St. Quintin Meinill Brus

Plate 8

Above: 18thC Darcy shield on the south front at Hornby Castle

Top Left: All Saints Church, Aston. The centrepiece of the Darcy window

Left: Aston Church; The Darcy window, Darcy impaling Meinill

Below left: Inn sign at Wales

Below right: Inn sign at Conisbrough

The Osborne Family to 1800

Amelia Darcy, (Lady Carmarthen and Baroness Conyers), had brought together the two major families of Darcy and Osborne.

In 1775 Francis Godolphin Osborne bought the larger manor of Wales, South Yorkshire, from his father-in-law Robert Darcy, 4th Earl of Holderness, 8th Lord Conyers. The smaller manor was already owned by the Osbornes through Francis' father Thomas, 4th Duke of Leeds.

Francis and Amelia's son George, born in 1775, became 6th Duke of Leeds and inherited his father's estates on his death in 1799, having already inherited his mother's estates and the Conyers barony at her death in 1784. To fully understand the implications it is necessary to look briefly at the descents to this time of the Osborne family and Dukes of Leeds.

William Hewitt (or Hewet) was a wealthy merchant in London, and in the mid -16th Century was lord of the smaller manor of Wales. Living in nearby Kiveton, in a cottage just off Hard Lane on the Harthill road, was the widow Jane Osborne, nee Broughton, of Broughton, Cumbria, and her son Edward. Jane's husband had been Richard Osborne of Ashford, Kent. William Hewitt's regular visits to the Osborne cottage resulted in his taking Edward, then probably in his mid-teens, to London as his apprentice. Here, Edward rescued Hewitt's young daughter Anne from drowning in the Thames, and there subsequently developed a relationship whereby Edward married Anne and formed the ancestral base of the Dukes of Leeds.

Edward eventually took over Hewitt's cloth merchant business and was later knighted, afterwards becoming Lord Mayor of London. He and his son Hewet Osborne continued to buy land in the Harthill, Kiveton, and Wales area and they also held lands as tenants of the Darcy family, who held the larger manor of Wales. As might be expected between influential families there is evidence of squabbles both in and out of court over rights to lands between the Osbornes and the Darcys.

Hewet Osborne was more of a fighting man than a businessman and though knighted by the Earl of Essex, was eventually slain in an Irish bog in 1599. His son, a second Edward, lived at Kiveton Old Hall and married firstly, Margaret Bellasis, eldest daughter of Thomas, Viscount Fauconberg. Note that a younger daughter married John, 3rd Lord Darcy of Aston, at Harthill Church.

Edward's second wife was Anne Middleton, a widow nee Walmesley, and by her was born Thomas Osborne who became 1st Duke of Leeds. Edward had continued the policy of buying land, and in 1636 had bought the manor of Thorpe Salvin including Thorpe Hall from the Sandford family, for whom it had been built around 1570. (Fig.19).

Thomas Osborne held all the titles of the peerage in his ascendency and his positions included High Sheriff of Yorkshire 1662, Treasurer of The Navy 1671, Privy Councillor 1672, Lord High Chancellor of England 1673 and Knight of the Garter 1677. In 1673 he became Baron Osborne of Kiveton and Viscount Latimer of Danby (Cleveland). 1674 saw him further advanced to the title Earl of Danby and in the following year he was made Viscount Dumblaine, Scotland. The Cleveland connection at this stage should not go without comment, since there is a direct ancestral route going back from the Osborne family through the families of Walmesley, Danvers (Earl of Danby), Nevill (Lord Latimer), Latimer, Thweng (Lord of Danby), to de Brus (46). Another de Brus daughter married into the Fauconberg family as discussed in an earlier section.

As Lord High Chancellor, a position he held for 6 years, he was Charles II's

Fig 19

Thorpe Salvin Hall. One of the homes of the early Dukes of Leeds.

chief minister, and therefore highly influential. As the political tide changed in 1678, he became accused of high treason, was impeached, and spent 5 years in the Tower of London. After his release he was to hold important political positions under William III, but controversy and corruption were never far from his side, though in this latter regard he was no different from many of his contemporaries.

In 1688 as Earl of Danby he participated in the Revolution Plot to overthrow the Catholic King James II; in fact he may well have been the leading protagonist, and was accompanied as mentioned under the Darcys, by John Darcy, (son of 6th Lord Conyers), and the Earl of Devonshire.

Thomas Osborne was created Marquess of Carmarthen in 1689 and Duke of Leeds in 1694. The Dukedom is named after the city of Leeds, not after Leeds Castle in Kent, which has been erroneously reported elsewhere. Local opinion at the time thought he would become Duke of Pontefract, but he chose Leeds because of the growing economic importance of this town in his home County.

The Duke was very astute financially, possessing good business skills. Yet he could be vain and pompous and was known as "Tom the tyrant".

Although he resided frequently at Thorpe Salvin Hall and presumably some of the time at the old Kiveton Hall, in 1699 he had completed the new Kiveton Hall (Fig 21), a far grander building than its predecessor and more in keeping with his high status. He was succeeded by his son Peregrine, and in turn by the latter's son Peregrine Hyde, all of whom were buried at Harthill.

For a thorough biography of the first Duke of Leeds, see Andrew Browning's book. (51).

Peregrine Hyde's son Thomas married the sole heiress of Francis, Earl of Godolphin. She was the grand-daughter of John Churchill, 1st Duke of Marlborough.

This Thomas (4th Duke of Leeds), thereby acquired Godolphin House in Cornwall but soon partly demolished it, though it is now in private ownership and open to the public.

Thomas Osborne and Mary Godolphin had three sons, and it was Francis Godolphin Osborne, their surviving but third son who married Lady Amelia Darcy, 9th Baroness Conyers. Francis remarried after he divorced Amelia, having a son and daughter by his second wife. He died at his London house, 21, St. James Square, of erysipelas, a streptococcal infection, and is buried at Harthill.

An abbreviated table of descent is summarised overleaf:-

Osborne

Richard Osborne = Jane Broughton

Edward (d.1591) = Anne Hewitt (d.1585)

Hewett (d.1599) = Joice Fleetwood (d.1619)

Margaret Bellasis (1) = **Edward** = (2) Ann Middleton (nee Walmesley, d.1667)
(d.1624) (d.1647) Her grandmother was co-heiress of
John Nevill, Lord Latimer

Thomas, 1st Duke (1631-1712) = Bridget Bertie (d.1704)

Peregrine, 2nd Duke (1659-1729) = Bridget Hyde (1662-1733)

Elizabeth Harley (1) = **Peregrine Hyde** (1691-1731) = (2) Anne Seymour (d.1722),
(1691-1713) (3rd Duke of Leeds) dau. 6th Duke of Somerset
(dau. of 1st Earl
of Oxford)
=(3) Juliana Hele (d.1794)

Thomas, 4th Duke (1713-1789) = Mary Godolphin (1723-1764),
heiress of 2nd Earl of Godolphin

Amelia Darcy (1754-1784) = **Francis Godolphin Osborne** = (2) Catherine Anguish
5th Duke (1751-1799)

George William Frederick Osborne (1775-1838)
6th Duke of Leeds
10th Lord Conyers

Francis Godolphin Osborne
(1777-1850) created Baron
Godolphin of Farnham
Royal Bucks.

Mary Henrietta Juliana
(1776-1862) Married
1801,Thomas, Lord
Pelham, later Earl of
Chichester

Francis Godolphin Darcy-Osborne
(1798-1859) 7th Duke of Leeds
11th Lord Conyers

George Godolphin Osborne
(1802-1872) 8th Duke of Leeds

The Bellasis (or Belasyse) Connection

Keen observers of the story so far will have noted three references of marriages to Bellasis, or in its originally written form, Belasyse family. Their seat was at Newborough, now Newburgh, Yorkshire, and the links are brought together as follows:-

Sir Henry Bellasis (d.1624) = Ursula Fairfax, daughter of Sir Thomas Fairfax

Conyers Darcy = **Dorothy**
(1570-1653) (d. 1653)
4th Lord Conyers

Thomas Bellasis (1577-1653) = Barbara Cholmeley
Lord Fauconberg of Yarm
1627

male line
and barony

John 3rd Lord Darcy = **Mary**
of Aston (1579-1635)
His 3rd wife

Sir Edward Osborne = **Margaret**
(1597-1647) (d. 1624)

Thomas, 1st Duke of Leeds

Thomas Bellasis was created 1st Baron Fauconberg of Yarm in1627 and 1st Viscount Fauconberg of Henknowle in 1643.

This Fauconberg barony became extinct in 1815 with the death of the 7th Baron. As previously stated it has no connection with the earlier barony of Fauconberg of 1295, re-determined in1903 for the 13th Baroness Conyers.

The Bellasis family (Anthony Bellasis was Henry VIII's Chaplain) had acquired part of the Augustinian Priory at Newburgh which they incorporated in the later country house. Their rise in wealth and importance followed this and other acquisitions of monastic lands, resulting in the subsequent baronies.

George William Frederick Osborne, 10th Lord Conyers (1775-1838)

He was born in Grosvenor Square, London in 1775 and baptised at St. George's, Hanover Square, King George III being one of his sponsors.

He was usually known as the Earl of Danby till 1789, and then Marquess of Carmarthen until 1799. On the death of his mother Amelia in 1784 he succeeded as Lord Conyers, and would also have been entitled Lord Darcy had he been able to anticipate the Committee of Privilege's decision some 120 years later. He was summoned to the House of Lords in 1798 as Lord Conyers, the year the Conyers barony was confirmed to him by the Lords, and in 1801 took his seat as the (6th) Duke of Leeds. His other titles included Lord Lieutenant of the North Riding 1802-1838, Governor of the Scilly Isles, Privy Councillor 1827, Master of the Horse 1827-30, Knight of the Garter 1827. He was also Ranger of Richmond Forest and Constable of Middleham Castle. He had inherited the Hertfordshire manor and estate at North Mimms, but sold it in 1799. In 1797 at East Rainham, Norfolk he married Charlotte Townshend, daughter of George, 1st Marquess Townshend. Their family was as follows:-

Geo Wm F. Osborne (1775-1838)
+ Charlotte Townshend (1776-1856)

- **Francis Godolphin Darcy-Osborne** (1798-1859) 7th Duke, **11th Lord Conyers** = Louisa Catherine Hervey-Bathurst (1801-1874)
- **Conyers George Thomas William Osborne** (1812-1831) Killed accidentally at Oxford while wrestling
- **Charlotte Mary Anne** (1801-1836) = Sackville Walter Lane-Fox (d.1874)
  - ***Sackville George Lane-Fox*** (1827-1888) ***(12th Lord Conyers)*** = Mary Curteis

It would appear that the respective marriages of George's eldest son and daughter caused no little consternation at the time.

Lord Wellesley wrote to George on 7th April 1828, informing him as a matter of courtesy and information that the Marquess of Carmarthen (George's son Francis), had proposed marriage to Lady Hervey and she had accepted. Lady Hervey, a widow, and Lady Wellesley were sisters. The marriage took place just seventeen days later on 24th April at St. Luke's, Chelsea. It seems from this time onwards, father and son did not get on with one another.

King George IV was obviously close to George Osborne and wrote to him at Bruton Street in June 1826. The letter, starting **"My Dear Duke"** concerned the recent marriage of The Duke's daughter Charlotte to Sackville Walter Lane-Fox. The King perceived Charlotte to have married below her station, as he refers to this **"very distressing event"**, and the **"rash and thoughtless step which Lady Charlotte has unfortunately undertaken"**. He signs himself as **"Your very sincere friend"**.

It would seem that George may not have entirely shared the King's view, since he tried to have his son-in-law installed in the Office of the King's Household, and he was later to favour him in his will. However, Prime Minister Robert Peel rejected George's request on the grounds of protocol, stating he could not place **"a commoner"** in such a position.

George was a keen hunter and had a pack of hounds at Kiveton which were kept on the edge of his estate near a road which is still known as Dog Kennel Hill. He was also a prominent patron of the Turf and his horse Octavion won the St. Leger of 1810. He also had useful horses in Jenny Mills and Moonshine, the latter a grey by Grey Middleham that won the Champagne Stakes. Tarquin, another of his horses, was one of the few that have run a dead heat in a match, which he did with Sir Bellingham Graham's "Biscuit" at York.
N.B. A member of the Graham family who came to Norton Conyers in 1624.

George died in London at the age of 62 and was buried at Trinity Church, Osnaburgh Street, Marylebone. Harthill Church has a stained glass window dedicated to his memory, incorporating a fine coat of Arms (Plate 7). His widow, who was baptised at Marylebone, died at Hornby in 1856, and was buried at Harthill.

George, 6th Duke of Leeds, 10th Lord Conyers. Left: Detail of portrait. Below: Caricature (Private Collections/ Photos courtesy of the National Portrait Gallery, London)

Kiveton Hall

Shortly after his father's death in 1799, George started to dismantle the estate and grand mansion at Kiveton, built by the 1st Duke in 1699 on the site of the previous Old Hall. The Hall had been built to reflect the Duke's powerful political status and, as his country seat, would have complemented his important London property, Wimbledon House. Even in the time of the 6th Duke in the late 18th/early 19th century, Kiveton Hall was on the Society visiting circuit. Much entertaining of the local gentry took place, including the Prince of Wales (later King George IV), who came to see the Duke's horses. The Prince wrote to George from Aske on 24th October 1806 - **"I look forward with great pleasure to making my bow to you at Kiveton".**

The Duke was also interested in music, and entertained his guests with operas, as chronicled in a letter by Lady Caroline Wortley who was staying at the Hall in 1807 with the **"Newarks and the Foljambes"** (39).

Yet within 5 years the Hall was to be completely dismantled, being fully demolished by 1812. As Robert Darcy had done before him, George moved to Hornby Castle, described in The Complete Peerage by the phrase - **"he pulled down the ancient family seat of Kiveton, moving to the more magnificent Hornby Castle".**

The reason for the demolition of Kiveton Hall has attracted much conjecture and discussion. The 6th Duke's love of horse racing was well known and it may be that Hornby, lying close to the leading northern racing towns, was more attractive to him for this reason.

Fig 21

Kiveton Hall. The front, or westerly aspect, around 1730. See also Plate 4.
(Archives and Local Studies Section, Rotherham Central Library)

Certainly it would not be surprising for him to have a keen interest in horse-racing, since the Godolphin branch of the family some generations back had acquired the Godolphin Arabian, one of three horses from which all thoroughbred racehorses are descended.

Other reasons have been proposed for the dismantling of Kiveton Hall which include the following:-

a) In absolution of a gambling debt to George, Prince of Wales, which committed the 6th Duke (10th Lord Conyers) to pay a large annual sum as long as Kiveton Hall stood.

b) To escape the advancing encroachment of industrialisation from Sheffield and Rotherham, a view strongly supported by local people both at the time and afterwards.

c) Financial reasons. The expense of maintaining the two substantial properties of Hornby and Kiveton must have been tremendous. It is reported that Kiveton Hall was in a poor state of repair and represented something of a liability; in fact the Duke was already in the process of converting the Park into more viable farm holdings. Hornby, on the other hand, had only recently been renovated by his maternal grandfather, the Earl of Holderness.

Whatever the precise reason for the demolition of the estate, one outcome was a court case after the 6th Duke's death brought by his own son (11th Lord Conyers), who had married against his father's wishes, the estrangement lasting till the 6th Duke died. In his will he left his unsettled property, including his mansion in St. James Square to his son-in-law, Sackville Walter Lane-Fox, father of the 12th Lord Conyers. Consequently, his own son, the 7th Duke (11th Lord Conyers) was left with just the settled estates so the latter instituted a law-suit against the trustees and beneficiaries of his father's will, alleging **"acts of waste"** in dismantling the estate. References were made to the pulling down of Kiveton Hall's South Pavilion in 1800 and the cutting down of ornamental timber in the Park in 1808. The outcome of the trial in 1852 after several appeals was that the representatives of the 6th Duke were decreed to pay his son and successor £42,000 plus interest. Full accounts of the Park and Hall contents are given in Arthur Twibell's publication. (25).

As has been said before in connection with some of the old seats of the Conyers family, "not one stone is now left on another", and this also applies at Kiveton. All is not completely lost however, for incorporated into end walls of two modern houses on the site are twin oeil-de-boeufs, (Fig 22a) with keyed limestone ashlar which formed part of the Hall's basement floor, clearly visible on an engraving by F. Badeslade in 1730. (Fig.21).

The bole of the original trysting tree was moved to Mr. Mosey's garden lawn.

Additionally, the gate piers and scrolled buttresses at the entrance to the old farm house are re-used material, and probably formed the main entrance to the Park. The gates themselves are in Harthill Church where they appropriately form the entrance to the Duke of Leeds Chapel.

The move to Hornby did not entirely sever the Kiveton connection, for the Dukes of Leeds still owned the lands until they were sold in 1920. There are records of a visit by the 10th Duke to the Kiveton Park estate in 1901 when he planted a young oak on the site formerly occupied by the famous trysting tree of Sir Walter Scott's novel "Ivanhoe". About 200 tenants were present and they presented the Duke with a silver bowl as a Christening present for his 6 month old son. It was thought that this may have been the first return visit to Kiveton since the move to Hornby. The occasion was additionally marked by the company having luncheon in a large marquee at Lodge Hill, home of the Duke's steward, Mr. Mosey.

The occasion was utilised by Rev. Darley of Harthill to refute rumours that the 6th Duke might have pulled down Kiveton Hall as a result of losing a bet, and to promote the notion that the move to Hornby was to escape the drifting smoke of growing local industry.

Fig 22

Surviving features from Kiveton Hall.
a) Oval oeil-de-boeufs
b) Gate piers and scrolled buttresses
c) Gates, now in Harthill Church

Francis Godolphin Darcy-Osborne, 11th Lord Conyers (1798-1859)

He was born in London, and the baptism was registered at Hornby. Francis matriculated at Oxford in 1815. From 1817 to 1828 he was in the Army and at the time of his retirement he was Captain of the 2nd Life Guards. He was Tory M.P. for Helston 1826-1830, and in 1838 was summoned to the House of Lords in his father's barony as Lord Osborne of Kiveton, unusually not in the older barony of Conyers which had been allowed his father. From 1799 to 1838 he was styled Marquess of Carmarthen. He took his seat as Duke of Leeds in 1839. As a peer he voted with the Whigs or the Liberals.

In 1849 a Royal Licence allowed him to take the surname Darcy before that of Osborne. As mentioned previously, in 1828 he married against his father's will, Louisa Catherine, widow of Sir Felton Elwell Hervey-Bathurst. She was the third daughter and co-heiress of Richard Caton, a merchant of Baltimore, Maryland.

Politically, Francis was described as a Tory turned Liberal, and in 1852 Mrs Edward Twisleton says of him and the Marquess of Clanricarde **"about as ugly men, each in his own style, as one would be likely to meet".** Compliments indeed!

Fig 23

Francis, 7th Duke of Leeds, 11th Lord Conyers. (Private Collection/Photo courtesy of the National Portrait Gallery, London)

Francis died of diphtheria in 1859 at the Clarendon Hotel, Hanover Square, London, and was buried at Harthill. His widow died in 1874 at the Roman Catholic Convent, St. Leonards-on-Sea, aged 81.

At his death, and with no surviving children, the barony of Conyers and the right to the Countship of Mertola (Portugal) devolved on his sister's son and heir general, Sackville George Lane-Fox.

The Dukedom of Leeds and the other honours devolved heirs male, and passed to his cousin George, whose descent is briefly outlined below:

Francis Godolphin Osborne (1777-1850)
(1st Baron Godolphin of Farnham Royal, Bucks.)

Sydney Osborne (1808-1889)	**George Godolphin Osborne** (1802-1872) 8th Duke of Leeds. Also Baron Godolphin. Born and died at Gogmagog Hills, Cambridge.
Sydney Francis Godolphin Osborne (b.1835)	**George Godolphin Osborne**(1828-1895) 9th Duke. Died at Hornby and buried in Hornby Churchyard.
	George Godolphin Osborne (1862-1927) 10th Duke. Died in London. Buried in Hornby Churchyard.
Francis Darcy Godolphin Osborne (1884-1964) 12th Duke of Leeds	**John Francis Godolphin Osborne** (1901-1963) 11th Duke. Lived in Jersey and France.
	Camilla Dorothy Osborne (b.1950) = Nigel Dempster

The Dukedom of Leeds therefore became extinct on the death of the 12th Duke in 1964.

The link with Hornby Castle and the Osborne family became broken at about the time of the 10th Duke's death in 1927. At this time it comprised principally four wings surrounding a courtyard with towers on all four corners, and was described in 1930 as one of the most sophisticated estates in the country (14). This was achieved mainly as a result of the work of William, 1st Lord Conyers, and Robert Darcy, 8th Lord Conyers and 4th Earl of Holderness. Peripheral service blocks had been built on by the Osbornes.

The 11th Duke placed the estate on the market, which was the first time it had been offered for sale since built, some 600 years or more previously. Shortly afterwards in 1930, when the estate had failed to sell as a whole, demolition was regrettably put in progress with the intention of selling off the architectural features and reducing the remainder to smaller proportions.

The major architectural piece that has been saved is a three-storey portal built by William Lord Conyers in the 16th Century. It contains a marshalling of the Conyers family coats of Arms supported at the sides by a carved lion and bull, surmounted by a coronet. This portal had been purchased by an American newspaper magnate, Randolph Hearst, with the intention of shipping it to San Simeon, California, but he died before the transaction took place. It is now on display in the Burrell Collection, Glasgow Museums and Art Galleries, along with the 14th Century arch from Hornby's entrance gateway and its 19th Century wooden doors. (See Appendix I and 2)

Since 1938 Hornby Castle has been owned by the Clutterbuck family. It is not open to the public.

Sackville George Lane-Fox 12th Lord Conyers (1827-1888)

The barony of Conyers (and that of Darcy according to the Committee of Privileges decision 1903) had devolved heirs general, and the 12th Lord Conyers was the nephew of the 11th.

The Leeds Dukedom, as mentioned, had devolved heirs male on the cousin of the 11th baron, so this was the first time since 1556 the Conyers barony did not have a shared peerage title.

The Fox part of the Lane-Fox family are readily traceable back to the 15th Century at least, when William Fox of Grete, Worcestershire, married Sibil, co-heiress of John de Grete. Their successors were Midlands-based in early successive generations.

Bramham Park. Home of the Lane-Fox family.

The Lane name enters at the marriage of Henry Fox to Frances Lane, Viscountess Lanesborough of Roscommon. Their son, George Fox-Lane, inherited the Lanesborough estates and he married Harriet Benson, daughter of Robert Benson. Benson had built Bramham Park, near Wetherby, about 1710 and was created Lord Bingley in 1713. Thus his son-in-law, George Fox-Lane, came to inherit Bramham Park as well, and he also succeeded to the title Lord Bingley. The Bramham estate then passed to George's nephew James, who turned the family name to Lane-Fox. James had three sons, the eldest of whom went on to inherit Bramham, where his descendents still live. The third son, Sackville Walter, of Oran House, Tadcaster, married Charlotte Osborne, sister of the 11th Lord Conyers. It was their elder son, Sackville George who came to be 12th Lord Conyers. Bramham house was badly gutted by fire in 1828 and remained empty until the early years of the 20th Century, so the 12th Lord Conyers would not have been directly associated with that place.

A brief descent of the family is shown below:-

Henry Fox = Frances Lane, Viscountess Lanesborough

George Fox-Lane = Harriett Benson
(1697-1773) Baron Bingley
by his father-in-law

Sackville Fox (d. 1760) = Ann Holloway

Marcia Lucy Pitt = **James Fox-Lane** of Bramham
daughter of 1st Lord Rivers (1756-1821)

1. George

2. William

Charlotte Osborne = 3. **Sackville Walter Lane-Fox**
(1801-1836) (1797-1874)

Elizabeth Catherine

Lora Mary

Charles Pierrepoint Darcy

Sackville George Lane-Fox = Mary Curteis
12th Lord Conyers (1841-1921)
(1827-1888)

Sackville Fitzroy Henry
(1861-1879)

Marcia Amelia Mary
(1863-1926)

Violet Ida Eveline
(1865-1929)

Sackville George was born in London in 1827, and baptised at Hornby. Though he lost his mother when he was only 9, he may have spent his early years at his father's St. James Square mansion. This had been bequeathed the latter by the 6th Duke of Leeds (10th Lord Conyers).

He entered the Army in 1854, the following year becoming Lieutenant of the 87th Foot, serving in the Crimean War. He received a medal and clasp for his valorous endeavours at Sebastopol, and took his seat as Baron Conyers in 1859. His right to the title Lord Darcy was not established till 1903, some 15 years after he died.

He held the manors of Wales from 1859 till his death in 1888. His ownership of lands both in Wales and Conisbrough would have led to the naming of public houses in those villages after his title.

In 1860 at St. George's, Hanover Square, he married Mary, 1st daughter of Reginald Curteis of Windmill Hill, Sussex, and Captain of the 1st Dragoons. They made their country home at The Grange, Wellesbourne, Warwickshire. This was a large early 19th Century house which they rented. It was next door to Wellesbourne House, owned at the time by Sackville's stepfather-in-law, Lt. Col. Campbell. In those days, Wellesbourne was a fashionable haunt of the gentry, who went there for the hunting and ball season.

In London, the family resided at 108, Queens Gate, a leaseheld mansion house with associated stables at 31, Mansion Mews, Queens Gate.

Their three children, a son and two daughters, were born in the early 1860s, but separation arrangements were initiated by Lady Conyers in August 1877. Significant financial provision was made on her behalf.

After his retirement from the Army, Sackville spent his time at various London locations. His townhouse was 17, Kensington Gardens Terrace, but correspondence was often addressed to his London Club, the Carlton, in Pall Mall.

The grass did not grow under this man's feet, as he stayed at numerous other addresses, notably "St. Clare", Walmer (near Deal in Kent), several in Ramsgate, and Paris. St. Clare was described as a **"fine mansion in extensive grounds"**, but like Wellesbourne Grange, it no longer exists. Towards the end of his life he also visited Brocklesby, presumably to see his daughter and son-in-law.

Sackville's financial affairs attracted much attention, generating a great deal of work for his accountants, legal advisers and those who administered his dealings. He probably experienced what we would nowadays refer to as problems of cash flow. Maybe his apparent inability to manage money

was inherited from his father who, despite the extensive legacy bequeathed him by the 6th Duke of Leeds, eventually became a declared bankrupt, and at one time owed his fishmonger £500!
Sackville himself left Wellesbourne with unpaid bills and a reputation for getting involved in legal disputes with his fellow local gentry. One such incident was reported in the Stratford Chronicle in October 1872. This petty dispute alleged **"insulting behaviour"** between Sackville and a member of the Liebert family. Refusing to accept a writ because Conyers' name was mis-spelt there ensued a confrontation at Conyers' wicket-gate during which he (Conyers) sustained a knee injury.

Two further items of personal trivia relate to his occasional suffering of gout and his membership of The Marylebone Cricket Club, though this is not to suggest there is any relationship between the two. In fact, he played cricket at Wellesbourne in the 1860s when the club became Warwickshire County Cricket Club. He also played for "scratch" teams such as the "marrieds" and the "eccentrics". The records suggest he may have been a better bowler than batsman, since he took more wickets than he scored runs.

There was a regular exchange of letters between Sackville and his daughters in the 1870s and 1880s, the daughters often being with their mother at Queens Gate. Correspondence increased around the time of his son's participation in the Zulu War in Africa. This only son, also Sackville, bore the family nick-name "Bag" or "Old Sack", while his daughter Marcia was known as "Mushie". Sackville junior had an unfortunate time in the Army, spending most of his time in the Field Hospital suffering from dysentery. It eventually killed him in October 1879, naturally causing great sadness within the family. He was 18.

Nine years later, in 1888, Lord Conyers died at Walmer and was buried there. His widow lived in London's Grafton Street thereafter. At the time of their father's death, Marcia had been married to the Earl of Yarborough for two years, but Violet was as yet unmarried. The sisters were always close friends.

The barony of Conyers thus fell into abeyance between the two daughters.

Queen Victoria terminated the abeyance of the Conyers barony in 1892 in favour of the elder daughter Marcia. The abeyance of the barony of Darcy (de Knayth) was terminated in 1903 in favour of the younger daughter Violet, who in 1890 had married the Earl of Powys at St.George's, Hanover Square, London. Thus the baronies of Conyers and Darcy are split, and the Darcy link proceeded as follows from the 15th Lord Darcy posthumously granted to Sackville George:-

Sackville George Lane-Fox (1827-1888) = Mary Curteis (1841-1921)

Marcia Amelia Mary
13th Baroness Conyers
(1863-1926)
= Charles Alfred Worsley
Anderson-Pelham
4th Earl of Yarborough
(1859-1936)

Violet Ida Eveline = Geo. Charles Herbert
16th Baroness Darcy (1865-1929)
4th Earl of Powys (d.1952)

Vida Cuthbert = Mervyn Horatio Herbert
17th Lord Darcy (1904-1943)

Davina Marcia (b.1938) = Rupert Ingrams (d.1964)
18th Baroness Darcy

Caspar (b.1962) Miranda (b.1960) Catriona (b.1963)

Debrett lists the current Darcy (de Knayth) residence at Maidenhead, Berkshire (26).

Wales

Several references have been made to the village's two manors and their ownership by the Darcy, Osborne and Lane-Fox families. Both manors eventually became under the ownership of Marcia, 13th baroness Conyers until her death in 1926.

It has been suggested that the Lane-Fox's may have seated themselves at Wales Court, but no corroborative evidence has presented itself. In fact all the evidence is to the contrary. An example is provided by Mary, Lady Conyers who writes to her husband in the 1870s. Their son, Sackville Fitzroy Henry, (Marcia's brother), had been throwing stones at his schoolmaster and Mary thought that he might benefit from spending time with a Mrs Kendall of Loxley or Mrs Fox of

Fig 25

Wales Court. Originally early 17th Century, now much altered.

Kineton. Both these villages lie close to the early family home at Wellesbourne, near Warwick.

Wales Court was originally a 17th Century building forming part of the Osborne estate. Sheffield Corporation bought the house in 1916 as a hostel, though it is now subdivided into several private properties.

Marcia Amelia Mary Lane-Fox, 13th Baroness Conyers (1863-1926)

Marcia was born and baptised in 1863 at Wellesbourne, Warwickshire, and in August 1886 was married at Cranley Gardens to Charles Alfred Worsley Anderson-Pelham, the 4th Earl of Yarborough.

Fig 26

Marcia, 13th Baroness Conyers. (Courtesy of Lady Diana Miller)

They honeymooned on the Continent and returned to the Yarborough family seat at Brocklesby, Lincolnshire. Here they were greeted to a grand reception. The railway station was decorated with bunting and the tenants escorted them from there to the Hall. At the entrance to the private carriage-drive, an evergreen arch of the foliage of yew and laurel had been erected, and fir trees temporarily planted alongside it. Her initials 'M', 'A', and 'M' were at the top of the arch, and the whole surmounted with flags.

This elegant lady, of dark hair and hazel eyes, had many literary and artistic tastes, including the collection of miniatures and other works of art. Her collections, with histories attached, were valuable additions to the established picture gallery at Brocklesby. She was herself fond of drawing and painting.

As President of the Needlework Guild for Lincolnshire, Marcia, or Lady Yarborough as she would have been known, reportedly received around 8000 garments a year for distribution. She also developed a great interest in district nursing in the Brocklesbury area, yet still found time for entertaining at their house in London, 17, Arlington Street.

Marcia became Baroness Conyers in 1892; just four years was the title in abeyance, and in 1903 she became

Baroness Fauconberg when that abeyance was terminated in her favour after an absence from the peerage of over 400 years. From her father's death in 1888 to her own in 1926 she held the two manors of Wales.

Around the turn of the Century, Marcia found another absorbing subject of study, something that started as **"a little amusement"**, yet developed into a time-consuming and fascinating project. This study (yes, you've guessed it) involved the tracing of the history of the Conyers family, their connections with the families of Darcy and Meinill, the collecting of pictures of Conyers tomb effigies at Sockburn, and the various armorial quarterings.

During the 1914-1918 War, Brocklesby was turned into a hospital for the wounded, all the cost of the equipment being met by the Yarboroughs. For her services, Marcia was awarded an O.B.E. in 1920, and she also bore the title "Lady of Justice of St. John of Jerusalem". She died, aged 63, of pneumonia following sleepy sickness, at Brocklesby, and is buried there.

The Church of All Saints at Brocklesby has a monument to Marcia; a white figure standing in a black marble recess, with two small boys clinging to her. (Fig.27).

Monument to Marcia, Baroness Conyers in Brocklesby Church.

It is reported that she brought 153 heraldic quarterings (familial coats-of-arms) into the Pelham family (40). 134 of these are identified and shown as an achievement of arms in A.C. Fox-Davies' Armorial Families, 4th edition 1902, and others can be found in Joseph Foster's Dictionary of Heraldry in the achievement attributed to Robert Darcy, 4th Earl of Holderness. This number of quarterings is considered a most impressive list in heraldic terms. It relates back to all the families entitled to bear arms as heirs, that were connected by marriage to the families of Fox, Lane, Osborne, Darcy, and Conyers.

In addition to being titled 4th Earl of Yarborough, her husband bore the titles 5th Baron Yarborough and Lord Worsley. In 1905 he renounced the name Anderson-Pelham in favour of Pelham alone, this latter surname originating from a lordship in Hertfordshire dating back to the Conquest. The name still survives in that county in the three villages of Brent Pelham, Furneux Pelham and Stocking Pelham.

Charles had succeeded to the Earldom in 1875 at which time he inherited the 50,000 acre Brocklesby estate. Though not always in the best of health, he was a keen huntsman and continued his family's tradition of tree-planting at Brocklesby. As with others in his family, he was a great benefactor to the town of Grimsby in addition to his involvement in rural affairs, and held the greatest respect of the Council there.

In 1907 Charles was President of the Royal Agricultural Society, and from 1921 until his death held the position of Hon. Col. the 3rd Battalion, the Lincolnshire Regiment. He became a Knight of the Garter in January 1935. During his lifetime (1859-1936), the agricultural depression took its toll which resulted in the leasing, then later the sale, of their London town-house in Arlington Street.

The nationally known Brocklesby fox-hounds had been sold, though later, in more favourable financial times, he restored the pack.

Fig 28

Marcia's husband Charles, 4th Earl of Yarborough

The Pelham family settled at Brocklesby in the 16th Century, and still reside there. The succession is represented opposite:-

Sir Richard Carew of Beddington, Surrey — William, Lord Sandys

Mary (1) = **Sir William Pelham** = (2) Mary

Sir Wm. Pelham (d 1587) = Eleanor, daughter of Henry Nevill,
(settled at Brocklesby) 5th Earl of Westmorland

Sir Wm. Pelham (d 1629) = Anne, dau. of Charles, 2nd Lord Willoughby of Parham

Sir Wm. Pelham (d 1644) = Frances, daughter of Edward, Viscount Conway

Charles Pelham (d 1692) = Elizabeth Wharton (his 3rd wife)

Charles Pelham (d 1763)

Mary Pelham (1677-1733) = Francis Anderson of Manby (1675-1747)

Francis Anderson (1711-1758) = Eleanor Carter

Charles Anderson, later Anderson-Pelham (1749-1823) 1st Baron Yarborough in 1794 = Sophia Aufrere (1753 -1786)

Charles Anderson-Pelham (1781-1846) 1st Earl of Yarborough(Worsley connection) = Henrietta Simpson (d 1813)

Charles Anderson Worsley (1809-1862) 2nd Earl of Yarborough = Hon. Maria Adelaide Maude, dau. of 3rd Viscount Hawarden

Charles Anderson-Pelham (1835-1875) 3rd Earl of Yarborough = Victoria Alexandrina Hare, daughter of 2nd Earl of Listowel

Charles Alfred Worsley Anderson-Pelham (1859-1936) 4th Earl of Yarborough = Marcia Amelia Mary Lane-Fox (1863-1926) 13th Baroness Conyers

Charles Sackville Pelham (1887-1914) Killed in action at Zandvoorde. Reburied at Ypres

Sackville George Pelham (1888-1948) 5th Earl of Yarborough 14th Lord Conyers

Darcy Francis Pelham (1892, lived 4 days)

Marcus Herbert Pelham (1893-1966) 6th Earl of Yarborough

Sackville George Pelham, 14th Lord Conyers (1888-1948)

The 14th, and last Lord Conyers (Plate 6), was born in 1888 and educated at Eton, and Trinity College, Cambridge.

He was 2nd Lieutenant in the Royal Hussars in 1910, Lieutenant in 1914, and Captain in 1916. He was awarded the Military Cross and mentioned in despatches in the First World War, though wounded at Vadencourt, France in 1918. In 1919 he had married Nancy Brocklehurst of The Spinney, Melton Mowbray, whose father was the younger brother of John, 1st. Baron Ranksborough.

He was styled Lord Worsley after his elder brother's death in 1914, till 1926. On the death of his mother in that year, he succeeded to the baronies of Fauconberg and Conyers, electing to be known as Lord Conyers.

Like his mother before him, "Sack", as he was known to his family, had obviously researched his Conyers title ancestry. In a 1938-39 photograph album kindly shown to me by his daughter, Lady Wendy Lycett, are several prints of a trip made to Sockburn Church.

Sackville had been a Major in the Nottinghamshire Sherwood Rangers Yeomanry in 1926, and Lieutenant-Colonel 1936-1940, serving in the 2nd World War from 1939 to 1944. In 1936 he succeeded his father in the Earldom of Yarborough, moving to Brocklesby from Harston, Leicestershire, and from that time until his death (7th February 1948), he was master of the Brocklesby Hounds. He died at Brocklesby, where his ashes are scattered in the woodlands as he did not wish to be buried in the mausoleum there. On his death, the baronies of Conyers and Fauconberg fell into abeyance between his two daughters and co-heiresses. At the time, there was press speculation that the titles might be separated, and inherited by the two daughters, but termination of the abeyances has not been sought. As there is no male candidate for the baronies, the title of L.G.Pine's book "New Extinct Peerages", (which lists Conyers), would seem to be appropriate.

The family is as follows opposite:-

Sackville George Pelham (1888-1948) = Nancy Brocklehurst
14th Lord Conyers

Robert Miller = **Diana Mary Pelham**
(d.1990 Zimbabwe)
(b.1920)
State Registered Nurse

June Wendy Pelham = Michael Hildesley Lycett Lycett of Morpeth, Northumberland. Major, Royal Scots Greys
(b.1924)
Served 2nd World War as 3rd Officer W.R.N.S.

Anthea
(b.1954)

Beatrix Diana = Simon W.J.Armstrong
(b.1955) (0f Gilgil, Kenya)

The Earldom of Yarborough devolved on Sackville's only surviving brother, Marcus. Brocklesby Church has a memorial to his elder brother Charles Sackville, who was killed in the 1st World War.

The Yarborough progression since then is as follows:-

Marcus Herbert Pelham (1893-1966) = Pamela Douglas Pennant,
6th Earl of Yarborough | dau. of 3rd Baron Penrhyn (d 1968)

John Edward Pelham (1920-1991) = Ann Duffin (nee Upton)
7th Earl of Yarborough

Charles John Pelham = Anna-Karin Zecevic
(b 1963) 8th Earl of Yarborough

Sophia

Arabella

Vanessa

George John Sackville Pelham
(Lord Worsley, b.1990)

William Charles John Walter Pelham
(b.1991)

James Marcus Pelham
(b.1994)

Margaret Emily Pelham
(b.1997)

Brocklesby Park

Fig 29

Brocklesby Park, late 1930's. (Courtesy of Lady Wendy Lycett.) *See also Plate 6.*

The earliest reference to a substantial house at Brocklesby is that made in 1697 by Abraham de la Pryme who described it as **"a very fine stately building, built in the year 1603 ..."**. (42). It was rebuilt between 1710 and 1730 and subsequently had several extensions, including an east hall by Capability Brown in 1772, a picture gallery in 1807, and another west block about twenty years later. In 1858 William Burn added two storeys above the gallery, which then became the drawing room.

Much of the house was destroyed by fire, believed to have originated from a chimney fire, in March 1898.

Sir Reginald Blomfield was employed to reconstruct the main block of the building, though parts not completely destroyed were rebuilt as previously. In 1956, the 6th Earl (Lord Conyers' brother), reduced the size of the house to very much the 1710 block, plus the gallery. Most of the interior of the present house is Blomfield's work, though Brown's east hall has survived. The house is not open to the public.

Brocklesby now stands in a Park of 1000 acres, which is entered on the western side by a classical Arch set up by tenants in memory of the 2nd Earl of Yarborough. Throughout the estate there are other buildings of architectural and historical interest, one of the most important being the mausoleum. This is situated at Great Limber and is believed to stand on the site of an ancient Roman burial ground. Designed by James Wyatt, a principal architect of the time, the mausoleum is based on the temples of Vesta, at Tivoli and Rome, and it is generally regarded as Wyatt's masterpiece. It was begun in 1787 and consecrated in 1794 in memory of Sophia Aufrere, wife of the 1st Baron Yarborough. She had died in 1786 at the age of thirty-three.

Between 1787 and 1823, twelve and a half million trees (12,552,700 to be more accurate) were planted on the Yarborough estate, and this was commemorated by the erection of Pelham's Pillar at Cabourne, near Caistor. Here, in 1842, Charles Anderson Pelham employed the Lincolnshire architect E.J. Willson to erect a pillar 128 feet high. It was completed in 1849 in time for a visit by Prince Albert.

Other significant buildings on the estate include the Conservatory, probably the work of Wyatt, the Orangery, stables, kennels, and 18th Century temples dedicated to Arabella Aufrere and Mary Carter.

The park landscaping was masterminded by Capability Brown during his two stays at Brocklesby in 1770 and 1772. Tree planting and felling is a continuous process here, many of the trees being introduced for experiment, but all meticulously recorded in respect of age and condition. Between the erection of Pelham's Pillar (1849) and 1932, twenty million trees were planted to form 3,500 acres of woodland with 193 types of trees and 89 miles of fencing.

The Brocklesby estate, as reported in 1991, consists of the Park, twenty seven and a half thousand acres with more than forty farms, and property in Grimsby. It also houses one of the finest private art collections in Britain, some of it inherited, yet assembled over many years.

Brocklesby Church.

Brocklesby Church

The Church stands within the Park and is dedicated to All Saints.
As seen today it is almost entirely 14th Century, though the North and South porches are 18th Century additions. The exterior is distinguished by a lead-covered timber spire. In addition to the fine monument and tomb of the first two Sir William Pelhams, the Church houses monuments to Marcia, 13th Baroness Conyers and to Charles, her eldest son.

It seems fitting to conclude the narrative by relating the inscriptions a) on Marcia's monument, and b) on the polished Ancaster stone font which is a memorial to Sackville George, 14th Baron Conyers.

Marcia

**"To the Glory of God
and in loving Memory of Marcia
Countess of Yarborough Baroness
Fauconberg and Conyers
who departed this life November
17th 1926 Aged 63 years.**

**A devoted wife, a loving mother,
a constant friend,
Beautiful, wise, and gracious.
Her ever ready sympathy
and unselfishness won the hearts
of all who knew her".**

The 'Last' Lord Conyers

**"For Mercy Courage Kindness Mirth
There is no measure upon Earth
For the spirit born to bless
Lives but in its own excess".**

Appendix

Appendix 1

Hornby

THE CASTLE AND GROUNDS

The preceding pages have produced frequent reference to Hornby Castle, which is not surprising since all but the last three of the 14 incumbents of the barony of Conyers owned it, and most of those lived there. It seems appropriate therefore, to bring together the elements previously reported and present them as one, together with additional detail where relevant. Notwithstanding the importance of Aston Hall as being a primary residence for the last three Earls of Holderness (Lords Conyers 6-8), Kiveton Hall and various London properties, Hornby must be regarded as the principal family seat of the first eleven to hold the Conyers title.

Situated in North Yorkshire a few miles north-west of Bedale, the hamlet of Hornby is dominated by its parklands and Castle, which stands on a plateau just south of the minor road that connects the villages of Hackforth and Arrathorne.

The Castle is usually reported as having been built in the 14th Century for the St.Quintin family, who were then lords of the manor of Hornby, and at this time it would probably have had just the one tower. However, there is a reference (43) to the Castle being of Norman origin, and the main entrance, facing south, dated at 1230. It is quite probable that there was a fortification here in Norman times which became owned by the St.Quintin family.

The structure was considerably extended by William, 1st Lord Conyers, in the late 15th Century, and in the 1600s the traveller/writer John Leland in complimenting William's work says that **"it was before but a meane thing."** (15)

William's extensions to the Castle resulted in a large courtyard plan with the principal frontage towards the south, overlooking the park from its elevated position. The keep that he built is at the south-east angle and the St.Quintin Tower was at the north-west. These two principal towers stood above the general level of the house and were somewhat taller than the other two angle towers at the north-east and south-west corners. The building was mainly of two stories, the corner towers of three stories, and what remains today is essentially the framework built by the 1st Lord Conyers. Hornby was never intended to be one of those grand fortifications as evident at nearby Richmond and Middleham Castles; it was not built solely as a defensive structure in times of war, but was more of a grand fortified manor house with no want of attention to domestic comfort.

The oldest part of the Castle was the St.Quintin tower and to its east ran the early 16th Century north range which was very much altered in the 18th Century. The large entrance gateway in the south range adjoining the keep, and forming the principal entrance into the courtyard, is regarded by most sources to be of 15th Century origin. So is the keep itself, albeit substantially restored and modernised. The carved trefoil to the keep's exterior represents a badge or crest of Conyers of Hornby, not their main one which was an eagle's wing, but a secondary one possibly adopted from the Melton family who had the same badge, and were related just before Hornby came to Conyers.

Hornby Castle Trefoil.

The north range contained the principal doorway from the courtyard to the great hall and was the early 16th Century work of William Lord Conyers. The doorway is now described as the Hornby portal and fortunately is in preservation as part of the Burrell Collection at Glasgow Museums and Art Galleries, which also houses the sandstone arch and oak doors from the main entrance opposite.

Entrance arch & doors preserved at The Burrell Collection.

Entrance archway at Hornby Castle.

The portal itself (Fig.34), is made of local Yorkshire sandstone and is the largest of the architectural stonework items in the Burrell Collection. It was dismantled at Hornby in 1930, and purchased for the Burrell Collection in 1954 from the vast store formed by the legendary American newspaper proprietor William Randolph Hearst, or "Citizen Kane". He had acquired many architectural pieces before the 2nd World War with the unfulfilled aim of re-erecting them at his fairytale residence in San Simeon, California. Prior to its purchase for the Burrell Collection, the portal is said to have been at Low Hall, Steeton,

Yorkshire, in a summer-house there, having been purchased by the owner Mr. Alexander Keighley, from a builder who was unaware of its origin. Being typical of many early Tudor monumental entrances, it is paralleled by a number of contemporary gateways to Oxford and Cambridge colleges. Its size is 23 ft x 8ft (6.86m x 2.29m). The heraldic devices in the portal are described in Appendix 2.

Fig 34

Hornby Portal, when in situ at Hornby. c.1900. See also Plate 7.

In the early part of the 18th Century Hornby was probably not occupied by the Darcys, since they had inherited Aston Hall from the older branch of their family. Nevertheless, the 3rd Earl of Holderness (7th Lord Conyers) started improvements at Hornby which were continued and expanded upon by his successor. The main work was to rebuild the south and east ranges with crenellations, hoodmoulds to the windows, and ogee arches to the tops of the window frames. A wing west of the St Quintin tower was also a mid -18th Century addition. By 1770 the 4th Earl was back at Hornby, and after he died in 1778, the Osbornes, Dukes of Leeds succeeded him.

Fig 35

Hornby Castle today. Site of portal.

They themselves added further service ranges and outbuildings. The internal arrangements suggest that the north side of the courtyard may have contained a medieval great hall, later divided by a first floor. To the west was a Georgian state room two storeys high and also a banqueting room. The east range once contained a Jacobean long gallery, later divided into bedrooms, while the south range had a library and billiard room on the

Hornby Castle - Inner Court. Early 19th C. (Sheffield Libraries and Information)

ground floor and first floor drawing rooms. To the north of the St.Quintin tower was a Victorian bachelor's wing with small suites for single male guests and their valets, and a corridor for the use of traversing servants lay unseen underneath the courtyard.

Hornby's interior was adorned with many paintings and furnishings that had accumulated over nearly 600 years of continued ownership through inheritance, including some of the furniture from Kiveton Hall.

The Park at Hornby covered about 700 acres and was believed to be the work of William, Lord Conyers. A deer park was sited away from the house in the south-west, but this was later turned over to farming by the 4th Earl of Holderness who had a keen interest in the pursuit of agricultural improvements. About 1769, the writer Arthur Young visited Hornby and described it thus:- **"It is true magnificence: all the by-roads through his lordship's estate are admirably good, superior to most turnpikes."** Holderness wrote to Young from his Sion Hill house on 8th December 1769, describing the agricultural techniques used at Hornby, and demonstrating his considerable knowledge of the subject.(50)

The park landscaping project was masterminded by "Capability" Brown, the country's leading exponent of such work at the time. It continued from the 1760's up to the 4th Earl's death in 1778, and even afterwards when the property passed to the 6th Duke of Leeds (10th Lord Conyers). The work undertaken on behalf of Holderness involved the building of the three eye-catching model farms, Arbour Hill House, Home Farm and Street Farm, and the construction of three lakes which curl round the park like a river, one with an ornate tufa bridge across it. Later Dukes of Leeds added large decoy ponds for duck-ensnarement purposes.

Fig 37

Tufa Bridge in Hornby Estate.

In 1930, three years after the death of the 10th Duke, the Hornby estate was put up for sale, at which time it was described as **"one of the most sophisticated in the country."** (14). As it was not sold in its entirety, it was broken up into 127 lots, including the architectural pieces. The sale advertised 9 reception rooms, 5 bathrooms, 28 bedrooms, 10 servant bedrooms. The estate totalled 5,850 acres, including the 500 acre park, 22 farms, and the villages of Hornby, Arrathorne, and Hackforth. The sad demolition of most of the Castle is graphically expressed in local press pictures at the time (September 1930). They show the removal of pilasters from the dining room, windows and oak panelling from the Great Hall, and lead from the roof. Amazingly, the Ducal coronet and robes formed part of the sale of contents.

Hornby Castle, a Grade I listed building, is now predominantly a crenellated two-storey south range (Plate 5) as modernised by the 8th Lord Conyers (4th Earl of Holderness) and bearing his shield of arms, (Plate 8), together with its 15th Century original archway and keep tower. The Castle, gardens and estate, still privately owned, are well-maintained in the Hornby tradition, and demonstrate the dedication of those who live and work there. Interesting accounts of Hornby are referenced (13),(14),(15),(16),(37),(50).

HORNBY CHURCH

The Parish Church of St Mary has been referenced many times in the text, and naturally it has been the final resting place for many of the Conyers, Darcy and Osborne families.

The history of the Church dates back to the 11th Century when a western tower was added to a pre-Conquest Church. The nave, north aisle and chancel were built around 1180 and the north aisle widened about 1330. A south aisle was provided in 1409 by

John Conyers, the first of the name at Hornby, the work costing 51 marks.

The Church houses many memorials relating to the Lords Conyers, including the font provided by the last Earl of Holderness' wife which bears the inscription **"The gift of Mary, Countess of Holderness, 1783".** Her husband has a memorial on the north aisle wall. William, Lord Conyers provided a bell, one of four at Hornby, this bell having been recast in 1656 and 1793, and originally inscribed **"When I do ryng, God's praises sing. When I do tole, pray heart and sole."** (13)

Most of the Conyers monuments lie in the south chapel, an extension of the south aisle, and late 15th Century in origin. Its building was probably instigated by Sir John Conyers (d.1490) in conjunction with a member of the Mountfords, another prominent local family. Following the creation of the first Earl of Holderness in 1682 it became known as the Holderness Chapel and remained the family chapel of Hornby Castle.

The south wall of the chapel contains a large mural monument to Elizabeth Conyers, wife of Thomas Darcy and daughter of the 3rd Lord Conyers. This stone monument is dated 1578, six years after her death, and bears three shields. One shield is of Conyers alone (Fig.39), another represents the families of Conyers, St.Quintin, Ryleston, Fauconberg (quartering Brus), Nevill, and Darcy. The top shield represents the families of Darcy, Meinill, Tempest, Waddington, and Gateford on the left side, whilst the right side shows the shields of the families of Conyers, St.Quintin, Ryleston, Fauconberg (quartering Brus), Nevill, and Darcy.

On the floor in front of this monument are two alabaster figures whose armour and dress are late 14th/early 15th Century and therefore are likely to represent John (Pl 2), the first Conyers at Hornby, and his wife Margaret St Quintin. In the floor to the east side of the chapel are brasses, the oldest of which commemorates Christopher Conyers and his wife Helena Rylestone, Christopher being the son of the above John. An ornate wall tablet is dedicated to Frances Darcy (nee Howard) who died in 1670 and was the 2nd wife of the 6th Lord Conyers, while a further tablet records the deposit of the remains of Robert Darcy, 4th Earl of Holderness, in 1778.

Appendix 2

Conyers Related Heraldry

During the research of projects of this nature it is impossible not to encounter armorial bearings, and their study can be useful in the pursuit of local history and familial connections. The following notes make reference to heraldic evidence relating to the Lords Conyers and the families into which they married.

Armorial bearings may be simplistically regarded as consisting of four elements; the shield, crest, supporters and motto.

A) The Shield.

The Conyers family shield of arms is a maunch i.e. a lady's sleeve, and is an ancient emblem or charge dating back to Henry 1st. (1100-1135). It represents the sleeve and pendent lappet of the outer garment worn by ladies in the 12th Century, and probably found its way into heraldry because it was a common "favour" bestowed by ladies on their favourite knights to wear in battle or tournament (28). Not only was the maunch the charge of the Conyers family, it was also borne by the old families of de Hastings and Wharton, but always in different colours (tinctures in heraldic language).

Various forms of the heraldic maunch are shown, plus an example demonstrating the position of the hand.

Fig 38

Forms of Maunch and Location of Hand.

The heraldic terms for the common metals, colours and furs are related as follows:-

Or = Gold
Argent = Silver (represented as white)
Azure = Blue
Gules = Red
Vert = Green
Sable = Black
Ermine = Black ermine tails on a silver background
Vair = Fur markings of the grey squirrel

In the description of heraldic shields, the background colour is always described first, followed by the description of the charge and the tincture of the charge.

The earliest known Conyers shields of arms refer to those three very early Conyers settlements at Sockburn, Hutton Conyers and Norton Conyers, the respective descriptions being azure, a maunch or; azure, a maunch ermine; azure, a maunch ermine debruised by a bendlet gules (Plate 7). This last shield or coat is a differenced coat, signifying its derivation from the previous one. The practice of differencing was used to indicate a different or younger branch of the root family, although the eldest son could wear the precise arms of his father when his father died. It could take the form of different tinctures or additions to the main coat without loss of the coat's basic identity. It was also used to indicate illegitimacy, not on moral grounds but solely to indicate the bearer was not the true blood heir of the lands and properties, which were all important in medieval times.

The very original Conyers arms, therefore was either "azure, a maunch or" or "azure, a maunch ermine". Unfortunately it is not possible to identify which is the original of these due to the family in-fighting or "in-murdering" in the 12th Century (see section on "Early Pedigrees"), where it could have been that the original arms passed with the younger branch along with the lands (17).

Evidence collected by some Heralds in their visitations indicates a change in coats of arms over three successive Conyers generations in the late-14th Century; i.e. Robert of Hutton Conyers (azure, a maunch ermine), his son, Robert of Ormesby (or, a maunch azure), and his son, John of Hornby (azure, a maunch or). (See Plate 7).

With reference to the Conyers of Norton Conyers it is worth noting that, although they changed their name to Norton, they have retained their coat of arms "azure, a maunch ermine debruised by a bendlet gules" to the present date, though they have carried the title Lord Grantley since 1782.

Conyers of Hornby and the first three Lords Conyers bore the arms "azure, a maunch or", sometimes shown as being differenced with two crescents. The full description would have been "azure, a maunch or, with a crescent of the second surmounted by another gules". However, Tonge (34) describes the differencing as a "black annulet", and careful examination of the Hornby Arch Shield does appear to support the presence of an annulet.

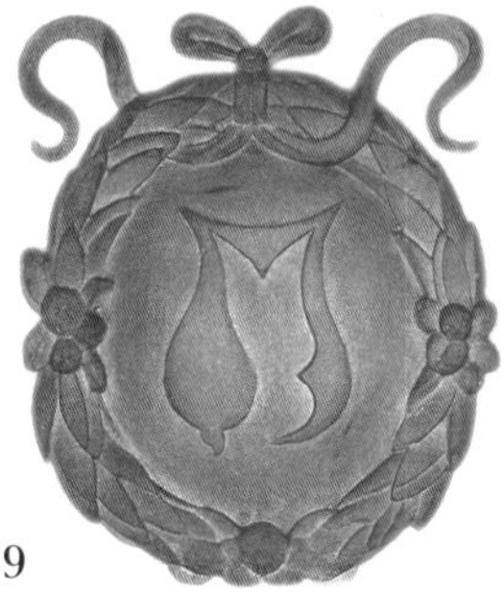

Fig 39

Hornby Church. The Conyers maunch on the monument to Elizabeth, daughter of the third Lord Conyers

B) The Crest

The earliest Conyers crest identified in The General Armory (29) is for Conyers of Sockburn and is "a trefoil slipped and erect vert" while Conyers of Hornby Castle is identified as the eagle's wing, "a sinister wing gules". The latter is the crest primarily associated with the Lords Conyers, but the use of a trefoil as a secondary crest at Hornby has already been mentioned under the section on Hornby Castle. Other Conyers crests are a Moor's head (Norton Conyers), a bull's head pierced through the neck with an arrow (Conyers of Essex), and a spear broken in three places.

C) The Supporters

William, 1st Lord Conyers, used a lion and a bull as the supporters of his achievement of arms, as exemplified in the Hornby Arch of the Burrell Collection at Glasgow. At Sockburn the 16th Century arms of Thomas Conyers bore two foxes as supporters.

D) The Motto

The Conyers motto was "One God One King", usually represented as "Ung Dieu Ung Roy" or "Un Dieu Un Roi".

THE HORNBY PORTAL SHIELDS OF ARMS (see plate 7)

The main shield forms the focal point of the portal which contained the main doorway from the courtyard at Hornby Castle into the north range. It was built by William, 1st Lord Conyers who lived from 1468 to 1524.

The shield, supported by a lion and a bull, comprises an achievement of nine familial shields of arms, assimilated in three rows of three. They are as follows:-

1. Conyers
2. Aton / Vesey
3. St. Quintin
4. Ryleston
5. Darcy
6. Meinill
7. Nevill
8. Fauconberg
9. Brus

1. Conyers

Azure, a maunch or, an annulet sable for difference.

The centre of the maunch (a lady's sleeve), is carved with an "annulet", a heraldic device used for differentiation purposes between family branches or members. Conyers of Hornby often used to "difference" with a black annulet, though there are references to red crescents and a red roundel (a torteau), also being used.

2. Aton / Vesey

a) Gules, a cross argent
b) Or, a cross sable

This shield is the one not normally identified in the literature. It is a plain cross, and is believed to represent the Aton (or de Aton) family through the marriage of Sir John Conyers of Sockburn, Co. Durham, who died 1395, to Elizabeth de Aton, daughter of William de Aton. The Aton family had inherited the lands and titles of the Vesey family through an earlier marriage, and sometimes used the Vesey arms.

Both families used a plain cross, and both have been recorded as using "gules, a cross argent" (a white cross on red), and "or, a cross sable" (A black cross on yellow/gold). The former is regarded as having the older precedence.

A description of arms at Sockburn Hall in the 17th Century describes the arms of Thomas Conyers in 1519 quartered with those of Vesey. Elsewhere, Thomas' son George, of Sockburn, is described as quartering his own Conyers maunch with "or, a cross sable"- obviously de Aton/Vesey.

A font cover is preserved among the ruins of Sockburn Church, and this bears a Conyers/Vesey shield in colour, the Vesey part being "gules, a cross argent". However, it is accepted that "or, a cross sable" was often recorded for Vesey in heraldic visitations, e.g. Flower, 1563-4.

The question why a Conyers of Sockburn family connection should be on a Conyers of Hornby achievement deserves examination, and takes us back to the section on Early Pedigrees, page 20.

The heraldic interpretation of the position of this shield i.e. next to that of Conyers, implies that it belongs to the family of the earliest heiress which Lord Conyers' direct ancestor in the male line had married. Thus the conclusion would be that Conyers of Hornby devolved from Conyers of Sockburn via John Conyers (died 1395) and Elizabeth Aton. This conflicts with the proposal put forward in pages 20 - 22 that Conyers of Hornby devolved through the Sockburn - Hutton Conyers - Ormesby link. Nor does there appear to be any heraldic evidence to support this latter view, though the weight of other evidence should still render it favourite.

William, Lord Conyers of Hornby, would have been building his portal around the same time as Thomas was living at Sockburn. Was William sure of his ancestry? Did he assume the Aton shield from Thomas? Maybe we will never know for certain, but it is worth noting the research has produced no reference or inference to any illegitimacy regarding John, the first Conyers at Hornby.

N.B. A further consideration that may have taxed past writers is the supposition in some heraldic visitations (viz. Tonge, Flower), that the first Conyers of Hornby was the son of Joan Melton and Robert Conyers. The Melton arms were also a cross, but always described as "a cross patonce voided." Considering the fine detail in place on the shields, such refinement to render the cross "patonce" and "voided" (as opposed to plain), would easily have been achievable. Therefore, the Melton consideration can probably be discounted in terms of the second shield.

3. St.Quintin
Or, a chevron gules and a chief vair, a martlet for difference.
The martlet (a heraldic swallow or martin), is engraved on the chevron. John Conyers, the first of the name at Hornby, married Margaret, daughter of Anthony St. Quintin of Hornby Castle, and inherited the estates.

4. Ryleston
Sable, a saltire argent, a crescent gules for difference.
Helena Ryleston was the first wife of Christopher Conyers, son of the above John.

5. Darcy
Azure, crusilly and three cinquefoils argent.
This shield is from the marriage of John Conyers, son of Christopher above, to Margerie Darcy, daughter of Philip, 6th Lord Darcy de Knayth.

6. Meinill
Azure, three bars gemel and a chief or.
This derives from the marriage, four Darcy generations back in the early 14th Century, of John Darcy to Elizabeth, daughter and heir of Nicholas, Lord Meinill.

7. Nevill
Gules, a saltire argent, a mullet sable for difference.
John Conyers in 5) above had a son, also John, who married Alice Nevill. She was the daughter of Sir William Nevill, Lord Fauconberg, by his wife Joan Fauconberg.

8. Fauconberg
Or, a fess azure in chief three palets gules.
The mother of the above John Conyers was Joan, daughter of Thomas, 5th Lord Fauconberg.

9. Brus
Argent, a lion rampant azure.
This is the shield for Sir Piers de Brus of Skelton and Danby, Cleveland. His daughter Agnes married Walter, 1st Lord Fauconberg. Their surviving son, also Walter, is believed to have assumed the arms of Brus in preference to those of his father.

Above the main quartered shield is a niche containing a stone carved with a lion, and above this is a shield of the Conyers maunch. To the far left are two more shields, apparently later additions, but possibly themselves being of earlier work.
These represent: (In the corner)

Dacre
Gules, three escallops argent.

This derives from the marriage of Christopher, 2nd Lord Conyers, to Anne, daughter of Thomas, Lord Dacre.

(Next to it)

Greystoke
Burulee azure and argent, three chaplets gules.

Anne Dacre's mother was Elizabeth, daughter of Sir Robert Greystoke. A chaplet usually signifies a garland of roses, as evident here.

GENEALOGY ASSOCIATED WITH THE HORNBY PORTAL SHIELDS

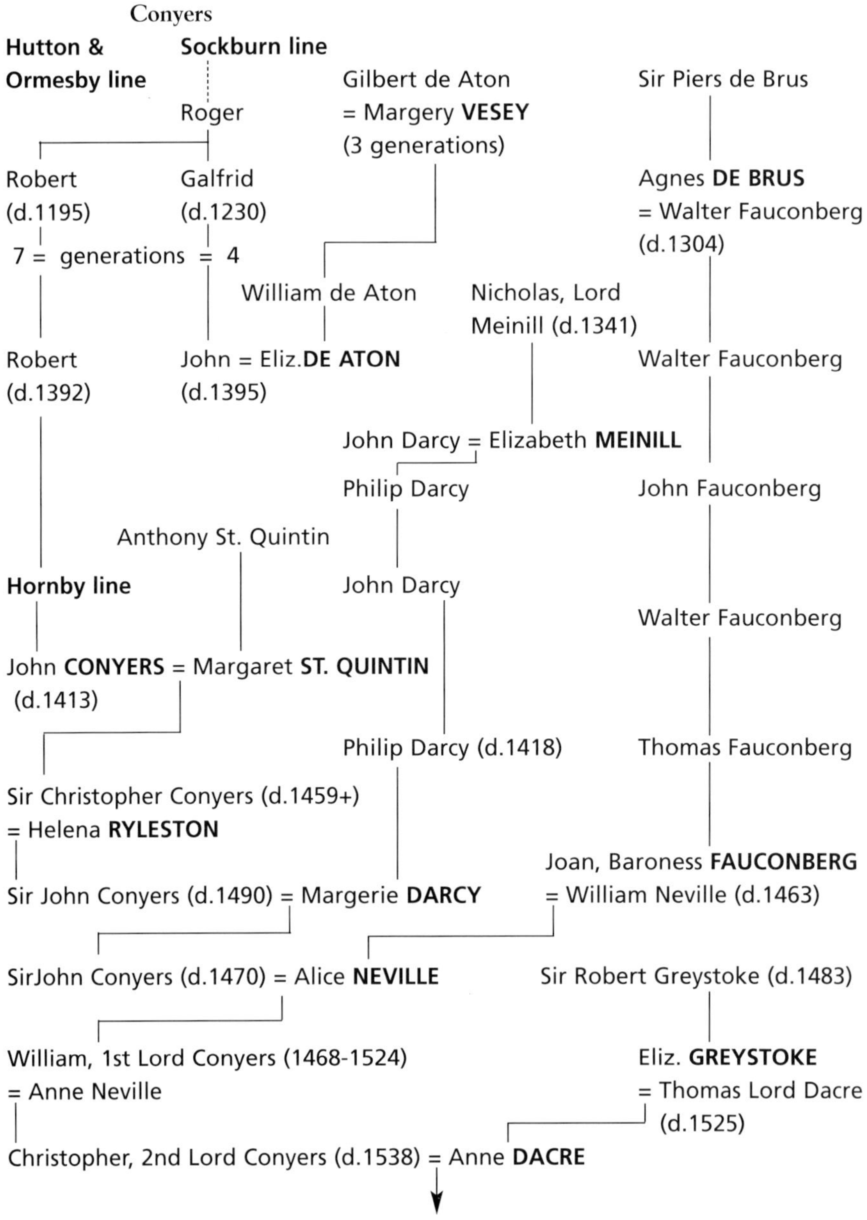

ARMS AT SOCKBURN HALL

Dugdale, in his visitation of 1666 (1), describes several shields at Sockburn including a group that formed an armorial window there. Many of these relate to Conyers of Hornby Castle family connections and include Nevill, Fauconberg, Scrope, Fitzhugh, Lumley and Dacre. Thought to have been located in the great hall and sculpted in bas relief are the arms of Thomas Conyers dated 1519, and the Conyers shield subquartering Fauconberg and Nevill, the Fauconberg representation being the adopted blue lion of Brus. As stated previously, the shield of Thomas Conyers is quartered Conyers and Vesey. Believed to have formed the armorial window were the following seven shields:-

1. Scrope and Tiptofte quarterly. Richard, 1st Lord Scrope (d.1403) held the wardship of Margaret St.Quintin of Hornby who was married to John Conyers, and he also held the wardship of the three daughters of Robert Lord Tiptofte (or Tibetot), who he married to three of his sons.

Scrope
Azure, a bend or
Tiptofte
Argent, a saltire engrailed gules

2. Nevill of Raby

Nevill
Gules, a saltire argent

3. France and England quarterly

4. Dacre and Vaux quarterly. The Vaux of Gilsland barony was transmitted to the Dacres via two heiresses.

Dacre
Gules, three escallops argent
Vaux
Chequy, or and gules

5. Fitzhugh. There is both a Sockburn and a Hornby link here, the former representing the marriage of Christopher Conyers, son of the Robert who died 1433, to Margery Eure. Her mother was Maud, daughter of Henry, Lord Fitzhugh. The Hornby link is via William, 1st Lord Conyers' first marriage to Mary Scrope, whose mother was Joan, daughter of William, Lord Fitzhugh - according to The Complete Peerage Ref. 19.

Fitzhugh
Azure, three chevronels in base interlaced or, a chief of the last.

6. Lumley. The above marriage of William, Lord Conyers to Mary Scrope produced two daughters one of whom, Elinor, married Richard, Lord Lumley of Lumley Castle.

Lumley
Argent, a fess gules between three popinjays (parrots) proper.

7. Nevill quartering Beauchamp, Newburgh, Berkeley, Gerard Lord Lisle and Tyes, all Nevill familial links.

ARKSEY CHURCH

The Church in this South Yorkshire village has some interesting and old stained glass shields, some in the form of roundels, among which is one of Fitzwilliam impaling Conyers. It is intended for William Fitzwilliam and his wife Elizabeth Conyers, the daughter of Sir John Conyers (d.1490) and Margerie Darcy. The Fitzwilliam coat would be described as "lozengy, gules and argent." (Plate 7)

All this blazonry has been described, and as yet, surprisingly, no representation of the dragon-slaying Conyers and his fiery flying serpent, nor even his falchion. However, a later Conyers family did have the foresight to make use of this connection, and Burke's General Armory describes a crest of Conyers of Willow Bank, Fulham. It is described as "a demi man in armour proper, scarf gules, holding in his dexter hand a falchion erect, transfixing a dragon, the head towards the sinister also proper". The shield associated with this crest is the usual "azure, a maunch or", but with a representation of the gold medal presented to Lieut.-Gen. Charles Edward Conyers for his distinguished services at the Battle of Orthes. This battle was in 1814 but it is accepted that the unaugmented shield and the crest may be older, but even so, they did not feature in the original arms of Conyers of Sockburn.

Having described the Conyers arms and those of some related families, it is now necessary to describe the arms of all the ***Lords*** Conyers and their direct families, which is best done by the following table:-

Lords Conyers 1 - 3

Surname: Conyers.

Arms: Azure, a maunch or.

Crest: A sinister wing gules.

Supporters: A lion (dexter) and a bull (sinister).

Motto: Ung Dieu ung Roy.
One God one King.

Lords Conyers 4 - 9

(includes 9th Baroness Conyers)

Surname: Darcy.

Arms: Azure, semee of cross crosslets and 3 cinquefoils argent (cinquefoils ermine differenced for Earls of Holderness, Lords 5-8).

Crest: A spear broken in 3 places or, 2 in saltire the other in pale headed ppr. banded at the middle by a ribbon gules (for Earls of Holderness.)

Supporters: Dexter, a tiger argent maned and tusked or, sinister, a bull sable armed and maned or.

Motto: Un dieu un roi.
One God one King.

Lords Conyers 10 - 11

Surname: Osborne.

Arms: Quarterly, 1st and 4th, quarterly ermine and azure, a cross or (Osborne); 2nd and 3rd, gules, an eagle with 2 heads displayed between 3 fleur-de-lis, 2 and 1, argent (Godolphin). SEE NOTE 1

Crest: 1st. An heraldic tiger statant or, tufted sable (Osborne). 2nd. a dolphin embowed sable (Godolphin).

Supporters: Dexter, a griffin or ducally gorged azure. Sinister, an heraldic tiger argent ducally gorged az.

Motto: Pax in bello. Peace in war

Fig 40

Arms of the Lane-Fox family

Lord Conyers 12

Surname: Lane-Fox

Arms: (Fig.40). Quarterly, 1st and 4th, argent, a chevron between 3 foxes heads erased gules (Fox). 2nd and 3rd, argent, a lion rampant gules within a border sable; on a canton of the first a harp and crown or (Lane).

Crest: Out of a ducal coronet or, a griffin segreant sable.

Supporters: Two bears argent

Motto: Inconcussa virtus. Unshaken virtue.

Baroness Conyers 13

Surname: Lane-Fox

Arms: Argent, a chevron between 3 foxes heads erased gules (Fox).

Supporters: Two lions rampant azure.

Lord Conyers 14

Surname: Pelham.

Arms: (Fig.41). Quarterly 1st and 4th, azure 3 pelicans argent vulning themselves ppr. 2nd and 3rd gules, 2 belts erect argent, decorated with buckles and studs or.

SEE NOTE 2

Crest: A peacock in his pride argent.

Supporters: Dexter, a bay horse reguardant, charged on the body with 3 ancient buckles or. Sinister, a water spaniel dog reguardant or, charged on the body with 3 crosses flory, sable.

Motto: Vincit amor patriae. Love of my country exceeds everything.

NOTE 1

These are the arms often encountered following the Godolphin connection, but an alternative incorporates as the third quarter "sable, a lion rampant argent, on a canton of the last a cross gules" (Churchill). Plate 7 shows this latter shield and is taken from the Duke of Leeds' window at Harthill Church in commemoration of the 6th Duke (10th Lord Conyers). The third quarter represents the arms of Churchill by the marriage of Francis Godolphin to Henrietta Churchill, Duchess of Marlborough. Their daughter Mary married Thomas Osborne, 4th Duke of Leeds.

NOTE 2

The Pelham buckle in the shield is a charge of honourable augmentation awarded to Sir John Pelham in the reign of Edward III. This was for his exploits in battle at Poitiers and the capture of the French King, John.

Fig 41

The Pelham Coat of Arms. See also Plate 6

ASTON CHURCH

About 1767 the predecessor of the current Aston Hall was destroyed by fire, but a fine armorial window was saved, elements of which now form an east-facing window in Aston Church (Fig. 42). All the shields in this window relate to Darcy connections prior to the involvement with Aston of the Darcy/Conyers line from Hornby Castle. They take the form of eight Darcy impaled shields around a central shield of eight quarterings.

The impaled shields implicate direct male-line Darcy marriages and, in "window" order, are believed to be those of Darcy (Azure, semee of cross-crosslets and three cinquefoils argent) with Heron (Gules, a chevron between three herons argent), Grey of Chillingham (Gules, a lion rampant within a border engrailed argent), Langton (Argent, three chevrons gules), Tempest (Argent, a bend between six martlets sable), Meinill (Azure, three bars gemels and a chief or), Grey of Wilton (Argent, two bars azure a label of three points gules), Greystoke (Burulee azure and argent three chaplets gules), and Scrope (Azure, a bend or). Some of these are now quite faded but those involving Meinill (Plate 8), and Scrope, at centre-right and bottom-right respectively, are among the clearest.

The central shield (Plate 8) is Darcy quartering Bertram (Gules, an inescutcheon and orle of cross-crosslets or), Tempest (Argent, a bend between six martlets sable), ? (Azure, a chief or), Melton (Azure, a cross patonce argent), Lucy (Gules, three lucies haurient argent), Hilton (Argent, two bars azure, on the uppermost a fleur-de-lis or), Darcy.

INN SIGNS

South Yorkshire boasts two Lord Conyers public houses, the Lord Conyers Arms at Wales and the Lord Conyers at Conisbrough (Plate 8). The inn sign at Wales represents eight quarterings and it is evident that they derive from the Arms attributed to the 13th Baroness Conyers, as illustrated and described in "Armorial Families" by A.C. Fox-Davies; fourth edition, dated 1902. (Fig 43). The signwriter, however, has taken some artistic licence in the representation of these quarterings. For example, the Conyers maunch in the fifth quartering appears as a harp, and the arms of Schomberg in the eighth quartering are way off the mark, though admittedly complicated and difficult to represent. The eight quarterings are intended to read as follows:- Fox, Lane, Osborne, Darcy, Meinill, Conyers, Nevill, Schomberg. The sign at Conisbrough is, with the exception of the supporters, a faithful representation of the arms of Pelham, the 14th and last Lord Conyers.

Fig 42
The Darcy window at Aston Church

Fig 43
Arms of Marcia Lane-Fox. Eight quarterings

Appendix 3

The Lords Conyers Descent Summary and other Peerage Titles.

1. William Conyers

Lifespan: 1468-1524

Barony: 1509-1524

Other titles:

Principal seat(s): Hornby Castle

2. Christopher Conyers

Lifespan: ? -1538

Barony: 1524-1538

Other titles:

Principal seat(s): Hornby Castle

3. John Conyers

Lifespan: 1523-1557

Barony: 1538-1557

Other titles:

Principal seat(s): Hornby Castle

4. Conyers Darcy

Lifespan: 1570-1654

Barony: 1641-1654

Other titles: Lord Darcy and Conyers
Lord Darcy de Knayth (Notes A,B,H)

Principal seat(s): Hornby Castle

5. Conyers Darcy

Lifespan: 1598-1689

Barony: 1654-1689

Other titles: Lord Darcy and Conyers
Lord Darcy de Knayth
Earl of Holderness (Notes C,H)

Principal seat(s): Hornby Castle

6. Conyers Darcy

Lifespan: 1622-1692

Barony: 1680-1692

Other titles: Lord Darcy and Conyers
Lord Darcy de Knayth
Earl of Holderness (Notes D,H)

Principal seat(s): Hornby Castle,
Aston Hall

7. Robert Darcy

Lifespan: 1681-1722

Barony: 1692-1722

Other titles: Lord Darcy and Conyers
Lord Darcy de Knayth
Earl of Holderness (Notes E,H)

Principal seat(s): Hornby Castle
Aston Hall

8. Robert Darcy

Lifespan: 1718-1778

Barony: 1722-1778

Other titles: Lord Darcy and Conyers
Lord Darcy de Knayth
Earl of Holderness (Notes E,H)

Principal seat(s): Hornby Castle
Sion Hill Aston Hall

9. Amelia Darcy

Lifespan: 1754-1784

Barony: 1778-1784

Other titles: Baroness Darcy de Knayth,
Lady Carmarthen,
Countess of Mertola (Portugal) (H)

Principal seat(s): Hornby Castle
Aston Hall

10. George William Frederick Osborne

Lifespan: 1775-1838

Barony: 1784-1838

Other titles: Lord Darcy de Knayth,
Viscount Osborne of Dunblane,
Earl of Danby (to 1789),
Marquess of Carmarthen (to 1799),
Duke of Leeds (1799) (Notes F,H)

Principal seat(s): Hornby Castle
Kiveton Hall

11. Francis Godolphin Darcy Osborne

Lifespan: 1798-1859

Barony: 1838-1859

Other titles: Lord Darcy de Knayth,
Viscount Osborne of Dunblane,
Marquess of Carmarthen, Baron
Osborne of Kiveton, Duke of Leeds (G)

Principal seat(s): Hornby Castle

12. Sackville George Lane-Fox

Lifespan: 1827-1888

Barony: 1859-1888

Other titles: Lord Darcy de Knayth ,
Countship of Mertola (Portugal) (H)

Principal seat(s): Wellesbourne

13. Marcia Amelia Mary Lane-Fox

Lifespan: 1863-1926

Barony: 1892-1926

Other titles: Baroness Fauconberg
Countess of Yarborough (Note I)

Principal seat(s): Brocklesby Park

14. Sackville George Pelham

Lifespan: 1888-1948

Barony: 1926-1948

Other titles: Lord Worsley (to 1936),
Earl of Yarborough (from 1936)
(Note J), Lord Fauconberg (Note I)

Principal seat(s): Brocklesby Park

NOTES A. In 1641 two Letters Patent were issued stating that a) Conyers Darcy should be Lord Darcy and b) Conyers Darcy, Lord Darcy, should be Lord Conyers. This would have been understood as a joint barony although he was likely seeking the restoration of the old Darcy de Knayth barony, though this latter interpretation was not confirmed till the Committee of Privileges decision of 1903. As stated in the text the Letters Patent were lost. He took his Parliamentary seat as Lord Darcy and Conyers.

B. With the death of Anne Pennyman, the sole surviving Conyers co-heir, in 1644 he became entitled to the original Conyers barony of 1509.

C. He took his seat in his late father's barony of Darcy, later writs erroneously appending the words "and Meinill", this barony having fallen into abeyance in 1418 with the death of Philip, 6th Lord Darcy de Knayth.

D. He took his seat during his father's lifetime in the original 1509 barony of Conyers, yet was usually styled Lord Darcy and Conyers.

E. His usual styling was Lord Darcy and Conyers.

F. He was summoned to the House of Lords in 1798 as Lord Conyers.

G. He was summoned as Lord Osborne of Kiveton, though a note in The Complete Peerage expresses curiosity that he was not summoned in the older barony of Conyers, as was his father.

H. In 1903 the Committee of Privileges met to resolve issues under the Darcy baronies (see note A). It was held that the 1641 Patents were in fact determinations of the abeyances of the then existing baronies of Darcy (1332) and of Conyers (1509). Therefore Lord Conyers incumbents from 1641 to 1888 were adjudged posthumously to have been additionally titled Lord Darcy (Lord Darcy de Knayth to give the full title). It was also held that the barony of Darcy could devolve down the female line.

I. In 1888, on her father's death, the barony of Conyers fell into abeyance but was restored to Marcia in 1892. In 1903 the same Committee of Privileges referred to in notes A and H determined the barony of Fauconberg, in abeyance since 1463, in her favour. At the same time the barony of Darcy de Knayth was restored to Marcia's younger sister Violet Ida Eveline. The barony of Meinill, although petitioned for, was not allowed, the Committee holding that no one had ever sat in Parliament under that title.

J. In 1948 the barony of Conyers became abeyant between daughters Diana Mary and June Wendy.

Appendix 4

Marriages of the Lords Conyers and their Direct Ancestors

LORD	NAME	MARRIED
	Roger Conyers	
	Roger Conyers	Emma, daughter of Ralph Aslaby
	Roger Conyers	1) Mary 2) Basilia
	Robert Conyers	Mabilla (Note A)
	Roger Conyers	Hugelesia, daughter of Sir Ivo de Longvillers of Hornby Castle, Lancashire
	Robert Conyers	Alicia, daughter of Nicholas de Yeland
	Roger Conyers	Agatha, daughter of Ralph de Newby
	Robert Conyers	Margery, daughter of Nicholas Ward, lord of Sallay, Yorkshire
	Robert Conyers	Emme, daughter of Hugh de Hougrave
	Thomas Conyers	Isabella
	Robert Conyers	1) Joan, daughter of Sir Henry Melton 2) Marion, dau. of Sir Wm. Daniel?
	Robert Conyers	1) Juliana, daughter of Sir William de Percy 2) Alianna (Aline) de la Ley, widow of Sir William de Dalden
	John Conyers	Margaret, daughter of Anthony St Quintin of Hornby Castle, Yorkshire
	Christopher Conyers	1) Helena, daughter of William Ryleston 2) Margaret Wadisley
	John Conyers	Margerie (Margaret), daughter of Philip Darcy, 6th Lord Darcy de Knayth and Meinill
	John Conyers	Alice, daughter of William Nevill, Lord Fauconberg and Earl of Kent
1	William Conyers	1) In 1479 to Mary, daughter of John, 5th Lord Scrope of Bolton Castle 2) Anne, daughter of Ralph Nevill, 3rd Earl of Westmorland
2	Christopher Conyers	In 1515 to Anne, daughter of Thomas, Lord Dacre of Gilsland

3	John Conyers	In 1538 to Maud, daughter of Henry Clifford, 1st Earl of Cumberland
4	Conyers Darcy	In 1594 to Dorothy, daughter of Sir Henry Bellasis of Newborough
5	Conyers Darcy	In 1616 to Grace, daughter of Thomas Rokeby of Skiers
6	Conyers Darcy	1) In 1645 to Catherine, daughter of Sir Francis Fane, Earl of Westmorland
		2) In 1650 to Frances, daughter of Thomas Howard, Earl of Exeter
		3) In 1676 to Frances, daughter of William Seymour, Earl of Somerset
		4) In 1685 to Elizabeth, daughter of John, Lord Freschville of Staveley, Derbyshire
7	Robert Darcy	In 1715 to Frederica Schomberg, Countess of Mertola (Portugal), daughter of 3rd Duke of Schomberg
8	Robert Darcy	In1743 to Mary, daughter of Francis Doublet, member of the States of Holland
9	Amelia Darcy	1) In 1773 to Francis Godolphin Osborne, Marquess of Carmarthen, later 5th Duke of Leeds
		2) In 1779 to John Byron, father of Lord Byron the poet.
10	George William F. Osborne	In 1797 to Charlotte, daughter of George Townshend, 1st Marquess Townshend
11	Francis G'phin Darcy Osborne	In 1828 to Louisa Catherine, daughter of Richard Caton of Baltimore
12	Sackville George Lane-Fox	In 1860 to Mary, daughter of Reginald Curteis
13	Marcia Amelia Mary Lane-Fox	In 1886 to Charles Alfred Worsley Anderson-Pelham, 4th Earl of Yarborough
14	Sackville George Pelham	In 1919 to Nancy Brocklehurst, niece of John, Lord Ranksborough

NOTE A

Assumes the descent as identified by Harrison (35)

Appendix 5

MASTER PLAN - Lords Conyers Lines of Descent

CONYERS		DARCY		OSBORNE		LANE-FOX	PELHAM
Roger							
Roger							
Roger							
Robert							
Roger							
Robert							
Roger							
Robert							
Robert							
Thomas		John					
Robert		John					
Robert		Philip					
John		John					
Christopher		Philip					
John	===	Margaret	Richard				
John							
1. William		William					
2. Christopher		Thomas					
3. John		Arthur	George				
Elizabeth	==	Thomas	John	Edward			
		4. Conyers	Michael	Hewett			
		5. Conyers	John	Edward			
		6. Conyers		Thomas			
		John		Peregrine			
		7. Robert		Peregrine Hyde			
		8. Robert		Thomas			
		9. Amelia	===	Francis			
				10. George			Charles
				11. Francis	Charlotte =	Sackville Walter	Charles
						12.Sackville Geo	Charles
						13.Marcia ===	Charles
							14. Sackville
						Diana	Wendy

References and Bibliography

(1) Surtees, R, The History and Antiquities of the County Palatinate of Durham. Vol.3, (1823).

(2) Harleian Society Manuscripts MS 2118 Section 2 fo.39

(3) Simpson, Jacqueline, British Dragons. (1980).

(4) Wall, John, The Conyers Falchion. Durham Archaeological Journal Vol. 2. (1986).

(5) Beckwith's Pedigrees of Yorkshire. Yorkshire Archaeological Society, Leeds.

(6) Lindsay, Jack, The Normans and their World, (1974).

(7) Surtees, op cit p. 244.

(8) Sharp's Manuscripts No. 70. Dean and Chapter Library, Durham.

(9) Burke, Sir Bernard, Peerage and Baronetage (1980).

(10) Yorkshire Pedigrees in Manuscript from the Burton Constable Library.

(11) Yorkshire Archaeological Journal, xxi, 58

(12) Hopkinson's Yorkshire Pedigrees.

(13) The Parish Church of St.Mary, Hornby, North Yorkshire. Church description.

(14) Richmondshire Architecture, pp 121-125

(15) Whitaker, T.D., The History of Richmondshire. Vol. II (1823)

(16) The Victoria History of the Counties of England. Yorkshire. Edited by William Page F.S.A.

(17) Fox-Davies, A.C., A Complete Guide to Heraldry. (1993).

(18) Hunter, Rev. Joseph, South Yorkshire.(1828-1831)

(19) G.E.C. The Complete Peerage.

(20) Dugdale's Visitation of Yorkshire,

Dalton's Visitation of Yorkshire 1558, Surtees Soc.122

Hopkinson's Yorkshire Pedigrees

Visitations of the North, Surtees Soc. Vols i-iv.

Surtees' Durham (refs 1 and 32)

(21) Barnes, Philip, The History of Wales up to 1900, (1991).

(22) Aston History Group. Some aspects of the History of Aston-cum-Aughton.

(23) Garbett, H., The History of Harthill, (1950).

(24) Sproule, Anne and Pollard, Michael, The Country House Guide, (1988).

(25) Twibell, Arthur, Kiveton Hall: A Study in South Yorkshire History, (1989).

(26) Debrett's Peerage and Baronetage (1995).

(27) Goodman, Anthony, The Wars of the Roses.

(28) Milton, Roger, Heralds and History.

(29) Burke, Sir Bernard, The General Armory of England, Scotland, Ireland, and Wales, (1884).

(30) Harleian Manuscripts 4198. Yorkshire Arms and Descents.

(31) The Itinerary of John Leland 1535-1543, edited by P. Centaur (1964)

(32) Surtees, R, The History and Antiquities of the County Palatinate of Durham. Vol. 1

(33) Flower's Visitation of Yorkshire 1563-4, Harleian Soc. Vol.16 (1881).

(34) Tonge's Heraldic Visitation of the Northern Counties,1530. Surtees Society, Vol.41 (1863).

(35) Harrison, Marshal-General Plantaganet, The History of Yorkshire. Wapentake of Gilling West,(1885)

(36) Bowen, Rowland, Cricket: A History of its Growth and Development throughout the World.

(37) Country Life, July 14th 1906, June 29th 1989.

(38) Untermeyer, Louis, Lives of the Poets. (1960).

(39) Aspects of Rotherham, edited by Melvyn Jones. (1995). Chapter on Kiveton: Seat of the Duke of Leeds, by Brian Elliott

(40) Pine, L.G, The New Extinct Peerage 1884-1971, (1972).

(41) Walker, Violet W, The House of Byron.

(42) Leach, T.R, Lincolnshire Country Houses and their Families. Part 2.

(43) Bogg, Edmund, A History of Richmondshire: An Account of its History and Antiquities, Characters and Customs, Legendary Lore and Natural History, (1908).

(44) Bulmer's Directory (1890).

(45) Atkinson, Rev. J.C., Cleveland Ancient and Modern

(46) Graves, Rev. John, The History of Cleveland. (1808)

(47) Ord, John Walker, The History and Antiquities of Cleveland. (1846)

(48) Foster, Joseph, Pedigrees of the County Families of Yorkshire, Vol. III, (1874)

(49) Throsby, John, Thoroton's History of Nottinghamshire, Vol. II, (1797)

(50) Young, Arthur, Six months tour through the North of England, Vol 2 (1771)

(51) Browning, Andrew, Thomas Osborne, Earl of Danby, Duke of Leeds (1951)

(52) Telfer, Paul, The Legend of the Sockburn Worm (1991)

Acknowledgements

Many thanks are due to all those who have assisted with the research and production. They include:-

Mr and Mrs Clutterbuck of Hornby Castle

Mr T Pace, Churchwarden, Hornby

Ms Gatherall, Sockburn Hall

The Dean and Chapter of Durham

Mr Roger Norris, The Dean and Chapter Library, Durham

The Northern Echo

Vicars/Rectors of the Churches at Hornby, Harthill, Aston, Arksey

Lord Yarborough

Sir James and Lady Graham of Norton Conyers

Staff at Brocklesby Park

Major Michael and Lady Wendy Lycett

Lady Diana Miller

Mr C David Harrison, Knedlington Estate

Mr James Lomax, Temple Newsam

The National Portrait Gallery

The Courtauld Institute of Art

The Yorkshire Archaeological Society, Leeds

North Yorkshire County Record Office, Northallerton

Lincolnshire Archives, Lincoln

Sheffield Archives

Warwickshire County Record Office

Staff at the Libraries in Leeds, Rotherham, Sheffield, Kiveton Park, Aston, London, Northallerton, Darlington, Middlesbrough, Lincoln, Worksop, Durham, Warwick, Deal, Selby, Tadcaster

Mr George Lane-Fox

Mr Peter Bolton

Staff at The Burrell Collection, Glasgow

Mrs Alison Nicholson

Lord Conyers Morris Men and friends

Mr Anthony Munford

Mrs Joyce Cracknell

Yvette Nuttall

Oakleaf Graphics

Dunston Printers

Millennium Awards for All